Discover

ENGLISH

3

Workbook

with CD-ROM

IZABELLA HEARN

My Picture Dictionary

Radio

1 Separate the words and match (1–4).

radioshowsvolumecomputerwebradioshow

1 _____
2 _____
3 _____
4 _____

Discovery 101

② The Big Mix

Sports Reports

Talk Back

③ **Discovery 101**
Web Radio Show

④

2 Complete the puzzle.

		T				

T | ¹U | R | N | | U | P

T | ²_ | R | N | | D | ³_ | W | N

R | E | C | ⁴_ | R | D

S | ⁵_ | I | T | C | H | | ⁶_ | N

D | O | W | N | L | ⁷_ | ⁸_ | D

T

S | W | ⁹_ | T | C | H | | O | ¹⁰_ | F

3 What does Lily say? Complete using these words.

on   in   up   record   radio show
volume   computer   web radio show

Hey there! Switch ¹*on* your ² _____ and download the ³ _____ . Tune ⁴ _____ to *The Big Mix*, the ⁵ _____ for cool people! Turn ⁶ _____ the ⁷ _____ and ⁸ _____ the show for all your friends!

my words

Do you know more radio words? Write them here.

_____
_____
_____

Present simple

4 ☆ Circle the correct words.

Mia ¹**work** / **works** at the new radio station. She doesn't ²**work** / **works** every day, only on Mondays and Fridays. She ³**likes** / **like** quiz shows. Her quiz show ⁴**is** / **are** called *Schoolz Out*. She ⁵**has** / **have** a chat show too, but she doesn't ⁶**asks** / **ask** the questions. She ⁷**answers** / **answer** them!

5 ☆ Write five questions.

Does	Mia	ask like work answer	at the radio station? on Sundays? quiz shows? questions? jokes? after school?

1 *Does Mia work on Sundays?*
2 _____
3 _____
4 _____
5 _____

6 Answer the questions from Exercise 5. Use *Yes, she does* or *No, she doesn't*.

1 _____
2 _____
3 _____
4 _____
5 _____

7 Match the words and phrases.

1 clean   a ki**t**
2 play   b you**r** teeth
3 r**i**de   c your hair
4 brush   d **a** bike
5 d**r**um   e football

8 Finish the word. Use the letters in bold from Exercise 7.

I can play the g_ _ _ _ _!

Frequency adverbs

9 Complete. Use the adverbs *often*, *usually* and *sometimes*.

1 always   ✳✳✳✳✳
2 _____   ✳✳✳✳
3 _____   ✳✳✳
4 _____   ✳✳
5 never   ✳

10 ☆☆ Write sentences about Tom. Use the frequency adverbs from Exercise 9.

✳✳✳✳✳ be in school early	✳✳✳✳ be busy	✳✳✳ ride a bike	✳✳ complain	✳ miss a radio show!

1 *Tom is always in school early.*
2 _____
3 _____
4 _____
5 _____

11 ☆☆☆ What about you? Use the sentences in Exercise 10 and make them true for you.

1 *I am   in school early.*
2 _____
3 _____
4 _____
5 _____

Lost And Found

Past simple

1 ⭐⭐ **Write the past simple of these verbs. Circle the irregular verbs.**

1 buy   (bought)
2 go   _____
3 shout   _____
4 take (photos)   _____
5 see   _____

2 ⭐ **Complete the sentences with a verb in the past tense from Exercise 1.**

1 I _bought_ a new mobile.
2 I _____ DJ.
3 He _____ over the bridge.
4 I _____ his name.
5 I _____ a photo of him with my mobile.

3 ⭐⭐ **Order the words.**

Mia find I can't Oh no! my mobile !
1 _Oh no! I can't find my mobile!_ _____

Lily see last you When did it ?
2 _____

Mia don't I know. Tom's I went to after school yesterday .
3 _____

Lily saw it But I in your bag this morning .
4 _____

4 **Rewrite the dialogue in Exercise 3. Change the underlined words.**

Mia _____
Lily _____
Mia _____
Lily _____

5 ⭐⭐ **Complete with the correct form of the verb in brackets.**

James	Hey! When did you ¹*buy* (buy) that football?
Tom	I didn't ² _____ (buy) it, I ³ _____ (find) it!
James	Oh! Where did you ⁴ _____ (find) it?
Tom	In the park. I ⁵ _____ (see) some boys and I ⁶ _____ (shout), but they didn't ⁷ _____ (hear) me.
James	Did you ⁸ _____ (follow) them?
Tom	Yes, I ⁹ _____ (run) after them but they ¹⁰ _____ (disappear).

A few minutes later …

James	Look, Tom! Hey, is this your football?
Boy	Yes, it is! I ¹¹ _____ (lost) it yesterday. Thanks a lot!

6 ⭐⭐ **True or false?**

1 Tom bought a new football. *false*
2 James found a football in the park.
3 Tom saw some boys.
4 He didn't follow them.
5 The football disappeared.
6 A boy lost his football.

7 ⭐⭐⭐ **Add one more true and one more false sentence.**

_____
_____
_____
_____

8 ⭐⭐⭐ **Change the sentences so they are true for you!**

1 Last week I <u>went to the cinema</u> with my friends.
   Last week I _____ with my friends.
2 I <u>walked to school</u> this morning.
   I _____ this morning.
3 Last month I <u>watched a quiz show </u>with my family.
   Last month I _____ with my family.
4 Last night I <u>studied for an English test</u>.
   Last night I _____
5 Yesterday I <u> went to a café</u> after school.
   Yesterday I _____ after school.
6 Last Friday I <u>played football.</u>
   Last Friday I _____

The Magic Amulet

Making suggestions

1 Complete the text. Use the words in the box.

> sister   rainy   museum   bored
> skate park   Ancient Egypt

Max and Holly are brother and ¹*sister*. It's a ²_____ day and Max is ³_____. He wants to go to the ⁴_____, again! Holly wants to go the ⁵_____. There's an exhibition about ⁶_____.

2 Who is speaking? Max or Holly?

1 Why don't we go to the museum? — Max

2 I'm bored! — Holly

3 Let's go skateboarding! — Holly

4 Oh no, we always go to the skate park. — Max

5 There's a great exhibition about Egypt! — Holly

3 Answer the questions about the text in Exercise 1.

1 Is Max bored?   *yes*
2 Where does Holly want to go?
3 Do Max and Holly always go to the skate park?
4 What is the exhibition about?
5 Does Max want to go to the exhibition?

4 Play heads or tails. Write the questions and answers.

☺ Good idea!   ☹ That's boring!

Why don't we

Let's

How about

1 Why _____ ?
   ☺ _____
2 Let's _____ .
   ☹ _____
3 How _____ ?
   ☺ _____
4 _____ ?
   ☺ _____
5 _____ ?
   ☺ _____

5 Complete the phone conversation. Use ideas from Exercise 4 to help you.

Friend Hi! How about ¹_____ this weekend?

You   Good idea!

Friend Hey! Let's ²_____ on Saturday!

You   That's boring!

1 Money

My Picture Dictionary

Money

1 Complete the puzzle.

```
B  ¹A  N  K
    O
    T
P  ²_  R  S   ³_
       ⁴_     S
    C        V
W  ⁵_  L  L  ⁶_  T
    S
    H
```

2 Match the words.

1	money	a	tag
2	price	b	away
3	pocket	c	box
4	give	d	money

3 Now use the words from Exercises 1 and 2 to label the pictures.

4 Circle the correct word for you.

1 I **save / don't save** my birthday money.
2 I **spend / don't spend** my savings.
3 I **give away / don't give away** my pocket money.

Do you know more money words?
Write them here.

_____

_____

_____

Present tenses

1 ⭐ **Complete the text and match with the pictures.**

> ~~saves~~ puts know takes
> counts sitting putting

1 Lily ¹ _saves_ some pocket money every week.
   At bedtime she ² _____ the coins from her
   pockets and ³ _____ them in a money box.
   She doesn't ⁴ _____ how much she's got. She
   never ⁵ _____ it! Today DJ is ⁶ _____ on her
   keyboard, as usual!   ☐ D

2 "Go away DJ!"   ☐

3 "Oh no! What's happening!"
   CRASH!
   The money is on the floor, under the chair and
   behind the desk.   ☐

4 Lily is counting it. She's ⁷ _____ it into her purse.
   "Wow! I can buy a microphone with this!"   ☐

2 ⭐ **True or false?**

1 Lily is saving her pocket money.   _true_
2 She doesn't know how much she's got.
3 DJ is sitting on her bed.
4 Lily wants to buy a microphone.
5 Every night she counts her money.
6 She's putting it in her pocket.

3 ⭐⭐ **Write six sentences.**

	today.
I meet my friends	every Friday.
	now.
We're working on the radio show	at the moment.
	every day.
	sometimes.

1 _I meet my friends every day._
2 _____
3 _____
4 _____
5 _____
6 _____

4 ⭐⭐ **Circle the correct word.**

1 Tom's saving his pocket money **sometimes /
   at the moment / every month**.
2 They watch a DVD **at the moment / now /
   every Friday**.
3 She's reading a book **every day / sometimes /
   today**.
4 He buys a magazine **every Saturday / today / now**.
5 They're having breakfast **sometimes / every day /
   at the moment**.
6 I listen to the radio **now / every day / today**.

Talking Tips!

5 **Write the words in the correct spaces below.**

Believe chance! I no don't it!

2 _____

1 _____

State verbs

6 ⭐⭐ **Order the words. Tick the three sentences with state verbs.**

1 like | My | BMX bikes | friends .
My friends like BMX bikes.

2 French | learn | I | school | at .
_____

3 listen | to | music | I | pop .
_____

4 hate | I | spiders .
_____

5 fourteen | am | I .
_____

6 money | their | save | They | pocket .
_____

7 ⭐⭐ **Write the three sentences without state verbs from Exercise 6 in the present continuous.**

1 _____
2 _____
3 _____

8 ⭐ **Match the questions with the answers.**

9 ⭐⭐ **Complete the text about Bill Morgan. Use the correct form of these verbs.**

~~talk~~   want   wear   save   love   prefer   hate

Mia ¹*is talking* to Bill. Bill ²_____ to go to Ireland and ³_____ money for the ticket. He ⁴_____ discos and parties, and ⁵_____ bike rides. Today, he ⁶_____ his special T-shirt. It says 'Love me, ⁷_____ my bike!'

10 ⭐⭐⭐ **Read the sentences in Exercise 6. Change the underlined words so they are true for you.**

1 _____
2 _____
3 _____
4 _____
5 _____
6 _____

Chat Show Time!

1 **Mia** Today we're talking to Bill Morgan. He wants to go to Ireland and is saving for the trip. Is that right?

2 **Mia** So how do you save money ?

3 **Mia** Yes! You're wearing your special T-shirt today. Tell us what it says Bill.

a **Bill** Well, I hate discos and parties. I prefer bike rides so I don't spend much money.

b **Bill** 'Love me, love my bike!'

c **Bill** Yes, I'm saving for the ticket.

1 Complete and write.

Pocket Money Survey

Names: Tom **£**   Mia **@**

I get pocket money	every day	
	every week	**£**
	every month	
I don't get any pocket money		**@**
I get money for	good grades	
	housework	
	my birthday	**£**
	baby-sitting	
I spend money on	sweets	
	magazines	
	CDs	**£**
	DVDs	
	presents	**£**

Tom gets pocket money ¹*every week*. He gets money for his ² _____ too. He spends it on ³ _____ and ⁴ _____ for his friends and family. Mia doesn't ⁵ _____!

Countable / uncountable nouns and quantifiers

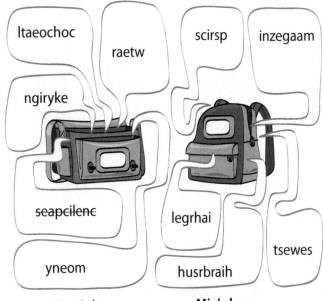

| ltaeochoc | | scirsp | inzegaam |

raetw

ngiryke

~~seapcilenc~~

legrhai

yneom   husrbraih

tsewes

Tom's bag   **Mia's bag**

2 ⭐ What's in the bags? Write the words in the correct place.

Countable	Uncountable
pencil case	_____
_____	_____
_____	_____
_____	
_____	

3 ⭐⭐ Write a sentence about each picture.

| There is
There are | a few
a little | coins
chocolate
crisps
water |

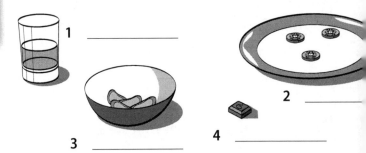

1 _____

2 _____

3 _____

4 _____

4 ⭐⭐ Look at the graph and complete the text. You can use the words more than once.

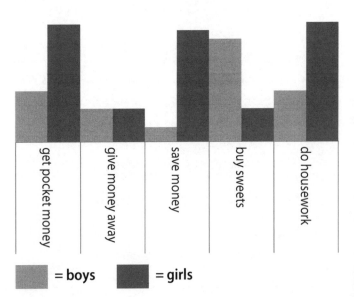

get pocket money | give money away | save money | buy sweets | do housework

▮ = boys   ▮ = girls

| much | a lot | a little | a few | many |

At Tom's school the boys don't get ¹*much* pocket money and they only do ²_____ housework. The girls get ³_____ of pocket money but they only buy ⁴_____ sweets. The girls save ⁵_____ of money and they give away ⁶_____ . How ⁷_____ sweets do the boys buy? ⁸_____ ! How ⁹_____ housework do the girls do? A lot or ¹⁰_____ ?

5 ⭐⭐ **Find and write four sentences.**

There crisps a isn't of There much lot are chocolate ..
1 _____
2 _____
There's few a little are sandwiches water There a ..
3 _____
4 _____

6 ⭐⭐ **Order the words.**

Lily Mia, I found your bag on the bus!

1 English bag the an is book there in ?
   Is there an English book in the bag?

2 any there Are pens ?
   _____

3 of Are DJ there photos ?
   _____

4 there Is purse a ?
   _____

5 there a Is library card purse my in ?
   _____

6 CDs any Are the in bag there ?
   _____

7 ⭐ **Circle the correct words.**

I don't get ¹**much** / **many** pocket money but I get ²**a lot of** / **many** money for my birthday. I usually get a few presents too, ³**some** / **any** clothes and books. I don't spend ⁴**any** / **some** money on sweets but I buy ⁵**a lot of** / **much** music CDs and magazines.

Simple maths

| plus | half | divided by | percent |
| a quarter | take away | equals | times |

8 **Write the words for the symbols in brackets.**

1 She got _____ in her exam. (60%)
2 He ate _____ of my pizza! (1/4)
3 I usually eat _____ . (1/2)

9 **Write these sums in words. Are the sums correct?**

1 $10 \times 5 \div 2 + 25 = 50$

2 $13 - 8 + 15 \div 2 = 10$

10 **Complete the missing number and write the sums in words.**

1 $6 + 4 \times 5 \div ? = 25$

2 $17 + 8 \times 2 \div 10 = ?$

11 **Write these sums in numbers. Are the sums correct?**

1 eighteen plus two minus five divided by three equals five

2 sixteen minus four divided by two times seven equals fourteen

12 ⭐⭐⭐ **Answer the questions.**

Do you get much pocket money?
_____

What do you spend your pocket money on?
_____

What do you usually get for your birthday?
_____

The Magic Amulet

1 Find the words in the pyramid and write them in the sentences.

UMYMM
MAELUT
HRAPAHO
RISHOGLYPHE
UAHORSPAGSC

The ¹h*ieroglyphs* tell a story.
It's about a magic ²a_____ .
The ³P_____ is looking for it.
The ⁴s_____ is beautiful, but the
⁵m_____ is a bit scary!

some- / any- / every- / no-

2 ☆ Replace the underlined words in the sentences below with phrases from the box.

> a guide / a shop assistant
> Egyptian mummies / jewellery from Greece
> at the cinema / in the museum

1 Holly and Max are <u>somewhere</u>.

_____

2 There is an exhibition of <u>something</u>.

_____

3 They are with <u>someone</u>.

_____

3 ☆☆ Write the words correctly and use them to answer the questions below.

> Where's Holly's purse?
> She is looking for it everywhere.
> There's nothing in her pocket. No one has got any money.
> They want to buy something. It's impossible! No chance!

oneon   hnmosetgi

wyvheerree   oignhtn

1 Where is Holly looking for her purse? <u>*everywhere*</u>
2 What's in her pocket? _____
3 Who has got money? _____
4 What do they want to buy? _____

4 ☆ Complete the words with the missing vowels.

Ev ¹*e* ry ²*o* n ³*e* is looking
Ev ⁴__ rywh ⁵__ r ⁶__ !
Ev ⁷__ ryth ⁸__ ng is dark,
There's n ⁹__ th ¹⁰__ ng there!
I can't see ¹¹__ nyth ¹²__ ng
Is there ¹³__ ny ¹⁴__ ne there?
There's n ¹⁵__ ¹⁶__ ne here,
Or ¹⁷__ nywh ¹⁸__ r ¹⁹__ !
Listen to the story,
Is it true?
S ²⁰__ m ²¹__ ²²__ n ²³__ ,
S ²⁴__ m ²⁵__ wh ²⁶__ r ²⁷__ ,
Has got s ²⁸__ m ²⁹__ th ³⁰__ ng for you.

5 ☆ **Complete. Use the words in the box.**

> ~~somewhere~~ everything nothing anything everyone something nowhere

The British Museum is ¹*somewhere* in the centre of London. The exhibitions are interesting for ² _____ . There is a big souvenir shop which sells ³ _____ . I always buy ⁴ _____ . There's a café too but I never have ⁵ _____ to eat. There is ⁶ _____ I like, and usually there is ⁷ _____ to sit!

Shopping

6 **Order the words in the dialogue.**

1 **Shop Assistant** you I help Can ?
   Can I help you?

2 **Girl** I'd please Yes, key ring like a .
   _____

3 **Shop Assistant** over got here We've some .
   _____

4 **Girl** one How is this much ?
   _____

5 **Shop Assistant** four It's pounds .
   _____

6 **Girl** I'll it take !
   _____

7 ☆ **Complete the dialogues with phrases from Exercise 6.**

1 *How much is this* pencil case?
   It's six pounds.

2 _____ ?
   Yes, I'd like a bottle of water.

3 This one is only one pound.
   _____ !

4 I'd like a T-shirt.
   _____

8 **Write the dialogues.**

1 You are in a café and you want to buy a drink and a cake. You have £10.
   You Can _____ ?
   Waiter _____
   You _____
   _____

2 You are in the souvenir shop. You want to buy a present for your friend. You have twenty pounds.
   Shop Assistant Can _____ ?
   You _____
   Shop Assistant _____
   _____

9 **Find the message.**

LOO KEVER YWHE REFORT HEAM UL ET

Pharaoh's Fun

Holly likes Egypt and she is going to celebrate. She is going to invite six new friends. They are going to have pizza and then a big cake. Holly is going to cut the cake into eight **equal** pieces. She is only going to cut the cake three times. How is she going to do it?

Reading

1 Read the text and complete the paragraph.

Give and Take Day!

5 September is a special day in West Woodhill. It's Give and Take Day!

What does that mean?

People can give anything they don't want or don't use and bring it to the Town Hall. Everyone has got something at home they don't use or don't want. Anyone can come, and take what they want! No one pays any money for anything, it is all free! There is always some furniture, and there are usually toys and books too. There are even a few computers and this year there is a printer. There aren't many clothes, and there aren't any shoes but you can often find bags and rucksacks.

The people of West Woodhill are busy looking in their houses and gardens, cleaning out cupboards … and finding treasure!

This year Haley Mason has another idea!

We can give and take skills too.
I'm learning to play the guitar and I want a teacher.
I can speak French and I'm good at cooking.
I can give an hour of French (or cooking) for an hour of guitar!

Anyone interested?

Contact: Haley
Telelphone: 0245 638 193

Give and Take Day is on ¹ _5 September_ in ² _____
People can come to the Town Hall and bring ³ _____
_____
No one pays ⁴ _____
It's ⁵ _____ ! You can you find ⁶ _____
_____
Everybody is busy ⁷ _____
Haley Mason had an idea! We can ⁸ _____
_____ !

Writing

2 Why not have a Give and Take day at your school! Decide on different skills that you can give and take. Look at Haley's advert and make your own.

What are you good at?
_____

Are you learning anything new?
_____

Design a card with the information!

I can give
_____

I am interested in
_____

Contact:
_____

3 Play heads or tails. Write sentences.

a Write down all the things in your bag on small pieces of paper and put them in a box.
a few sweets, some pencils, a _____

b Take a word from the box and spin the coin.

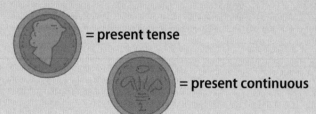

= present tense

= present continuous

c Write a sentence!

We're buying a few sweets with our pocket money.

Out And About

My Picture Dictionary

Transport verbs

1 Complete the words with the missing vowels.

1 p _i_ ck _u_ p

2 g _ t _ n

4 g _ t _ n

3 c _ tch

6 m _ ss

5 g _ t _ ff

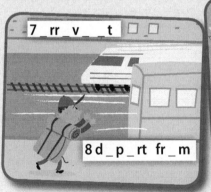

7 _ rr _ v _ _ t

8 d _ p _ rt fr _ m

11 t _ k _ _ ff

10 dr _ p _ ff

9 g _ t _ _ t _ f

12 l _ nd

2 Circle the words.

planetrainboatbuscarbike

3 Circle the correct words.

1 We get on our **bikes** / cars.
2 Don't miss the **bike** / **plane**!
3 I always catch the early **bus** / **car**.
4 I get off the **car** / **bus** at the shops.
5 Don't get in that **train** / **car**.
6 They get out of the **bike** / **boat**.

my words

Do you know more transport words?
Write them here.

_____

_____

_____

_____

Talking Tips!

1 Complete the dialogue.

> I don't believe it! No way! He's in a rush!
> No chance! hang on!

Gerry ¹*I don't believe it!* There's Gary Goalie!
Horace Wow! ² _____ _____ _____ _____
Both Hey, Gary, ³ _____ _____
Gerry ⁴ _____ _____ Look, he's getting on the
airport bus. That's our bus too!
Horace ⁵ _____ _____ Quick, run!
Gerry Oh no! It's going!

Present continuous for the future

2 ⭐ Read and complete.

> catching staying coming playing having
> seeing sightseeing driving visiting

Gary Goalie is ¹*catching* the plane to Milan on Saturday night. He's ² _____ at The Club Inn for two nights. On Monday he's ³ _____ in the match but first he's ⁴ _____ the doctor. All the players are ⁵ _____ a check up. They aren't ⁶ _____ , there's no time. After the match he's ⁷ _____ to Venice. He's ⁸ _____ friends there and having a few days holiday. He isn't ⁹ _____ back to England for a few weeks.

3 ⭐⭐ Order the words.

1 train Gary Goalie catching is a ?
Is Gary Goalie catching a train?

2 in staying a in he Milan is hotel ?
_____

3 doctor are seeing the players the ?
_____

4 they in sightseeing Milan are ?
_____

5 driving is to Venice Gary ?
_____

6 England the is back he to coming match after ?
_____

4 ⭐ Answer the questions in Exercise 3. Use these words.

> Yes, they are.   Yes, he is.
> No, they aren't.   No, he isn't.

5 ⭐⭐ **What's happening on Saturday? Write sentences.**

> Lily's plans
> 9 a.m. – pick up tickets!
> (Drop off DJ with Auntie Kay)
> Catch 11.30 airport bus
> Luton Airport – Edinburgh 2.30!
> Folk for Folk concert 7 p.m.

> Tom's plans
> 8.30 a.m. - pick up James!
> (Drop off keys with Uncle Max)
> Catch 10.00 train to Luton
> Luton Airport - Barcelona 12.15!
> Real Madrid v. Barcelona match 5 p.m.

1 Lily / pick up / tickets / morning.
   Lily is picking up the tickets in the morning.
2 Tom / go / airport / by train.
   _____
3 Aunty Kay / feed / DJ.
   _____
4 Uncle Max / look after / keys.
   _____
5 Tom / watch / football match / 5 p.m.
   _____
6 Lily's plane / take off / 2.30 p.m.
   _____

6 ⭐⭐⭐ **Complete the dialogues. Use Tom and Lily's weekend plans to help you.**

Mia What are you doing next weekend?
Lily Well, we're going to a ¹*concert*. It's in
      ² _____ !
Mia I don't believe it! Lucky you!
Mia What ³ _____ ?
Tom Well, we're ⁴ _____ !
Mia I don't ⁵ _____ ! Lucky ⁶ _____ !

7 ⭐⭐ **Order the words and answer the question.**

What do you think Mia is doing this weekend?

isn't She anything doing !

_____

8 ⭐ **Write six sentences that are true for you.**

I	'm 'm not		football	
		playing	to a show	next week.
My best friend	is	going	a party	tomorrow.
My grandmother	isn't	having	basketball	in the summer.
My friends	are		to the park	
	aren't		a picnic	

1 _____
2 _____
3 _____
4 _____
5 _____
6 _____

Inviting

9 **Order the sentences in the dialogue.**

Ana   OK. Maybe another time?
Ellie Sorry, I'm afraid I can't. I'm <u>playing basketball</u>.
Ana   What are you doing next <u>weekend?</u>   1
Ellie Nothing special.
Ana   Would you like to go to a <u>music festival on Sunday?</u>

10 ⭐⭐⭐ **Write your own dialogue. Use the dialogue in Exercise 9 to help you. Change the words that are underlined.**

_____
_____
_____
_____
_____

Transport Of The Future

will / won't predictions

1 ☆ **Read and match the text and pictures.
Do we have any of these today?**

1   In the future, trains will travel very fast, 300 kilometres an hour!
2   Soon, they will build a tunnel under the sea. People will catch a train in London, England and get off in Paris, France and they won't get their feet wet!
3   One day, there won't be any road accidents or traffic jams. People will travel in a large, round ball with big windows, called a rollerball.
4   In the future, planes will fly fives times faster than sound. A plane will pick you up in Brussels, Belgium and drop you off in Sydney, Australia about five hours later!

1   *C - Yes, we do.*
2   _____
3   _____
4   _____

2 ☆☆ **Order the words.**

The Rollerball

1   pollute It won't .
    It won't pollute.
2   very will It cheap be .
    _____
3   fly It won't .
    _____
4   go It fast will .
    _____
5   carry It 100 will people .
    _____
6   won't It a make noise .
    _____

3 ☆☆☆ **Ask and answer. Use the information in Exercise 2 to help you.**

Today Dr. Adams will answer questions about *The Rollerball*.

1   *Will it pollute? No, it won't pollute.*
2   _____
3   _____
4   _____
5   _____
6   _____

Verb to noun

4 Complete the verbs with the missing vowels.

1 e nj o y
2 _ rg _ _
3 _ nt _ rt _ _ n

4 c _ mp _ t _
5 _ m _ g _ n _

5 Now find the nouns.

im
en
ar
com
enter

gu
agin
tain
peti
joy

ment
ment
ation
tion
ment

1 *argument*
2 _____
3 _____

4 _____
5 _____

6 Complete the text.

(~~prediction~~ invite imagine discussion pollution)

Dr. Adam's ¹*prediction* is that transport will improve.
In the future there won't be any ²_____. Next
week he will ³_____ some school children for a
⁴_____ about his rollerball, his favourite invention.
Can you ⁵_____ rolling to school?

7 ☆ What will Dr Adam's family do to improve
the environment? Write sentences.

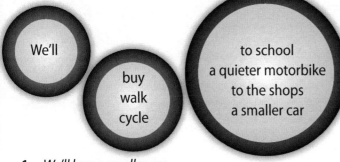

We'll

buy
walk
cycle

to school
a quieter motorbike
to the shops
a smaller car

1 *We'll buy a smaller car.*
2 _____
3 _____
4 _____

8 ☆☆☆ What three things will YOU do?

_____
_____
_____

9 Write three sentences about the SeaPhantom.
Include all the information below. Use *and*, *but* and
because to link the ideas.

The SeaPhantom

Only rich people will buy the SeaPhantom.
It will cost about $500,000.
It will go as fast as a helicopter.
It will fly too, above the sea!
The SeaPhantom will travel fast.
It won't pollute much.

1 _____
2 _____
3 _____

10 ☆☆☆ Imagine what will happen in 2040.

How will children get to school?
Will we have traffic jams?
Will transport be expensive?
Will there be any pollution?
Will robots drive our cars?
I think _____
_____
_____
_____
_____

Keep this book until 2040!
Were you right?

1 Write the words correctly and use them to complete the sentences.

> ~~itcnAine ytgEp~~ eautlm gmaic
> irmdyap ohaPrah fahl

1 Holly and Max are in _Ancient Egypt._
2 Holly is wearing half an _____.
3 It belonged to a _____.
4 It was _____.
5 Where is the other _____?
6 They are going to look in the _____.

going to

2 ⭐⭐ What are Holly and Max going to do? Complete the sentences.

	GO HOME	EXPLORE PYRAMIDS	LOOK FOR TREASURE	WEAR JEWELLERY
HOLLY	✗	✓	✗	✓
MAX	✗	✓	✓	✗

1 They are not going to _go home._
2 They _____
3 Holly is going to wear _____
4 She isn't _____
5 Max _____ jewellery.
6 He _____ treasure.

3 ⭐⭐ **What dreams did Tutankhamun have?**
Order the words.

1 going · be · to · a · am · powerful · I · Pharaoh ·
I am going to be a powerful Pharaoh

2 am · to · of · a · have · lot · camels · I · going ·
_____

3 I · build · to · going · pyramids · am ·
_____

4 I'm · to · kill · going · people · not ·
_____

5 not · my · going · to · treasure · I'm · hide ·
_____

6 wear · to · I'm · jewellery · going ·
_____

4 ⭐⭐ **You are interviewing Tutankhamun!**
Ask the questions.

1 what / be?
What are you going to be in the future?

2 have / cats?
_____

3 what / build?
_____

4 kill / people?
_____

5 hide / treasure?
_____

6 break / jewellery?
_____

5 ⭐⭐ **Now answer the questions in Exercise 4**
for Tutankhamun.

1 *I'm going to be a powerful Pharaoh.*
2 _____
3 _____
4 _____
5 _____
6 _____

6 ⭐⭐ **Read and answer the questions.**

Hi! I'm Cleo and I'm in Egypt this week. I'm going to help Dr Anthony look for mummies.

Cleo! Where are you! Look at this, it's Ramses! Look at all that treasure. We're going to pack it into boxes, OK? And we're going to send Ramses to Paris on a plane. Dr Nile is going to examine him for us. I'm not going to touch him. I don't want to break him!

1 Where is Cleo?   *Egypt*
2 Who is she going to help?
3 What is she going to do with the treasure?
4 Where are they going to send Ramses?
5 How are they going to send him?
6 Why isn't Dr Anthony going to touch him?

7 ⭐⭐⭐ **Add two more questions.**

1 _____
2 _____

Let's Revise!

Vocabulary

1 **Match the opposites.**

1 miss   **a** drop off
2 pick up   **b** arrive at
3 depart from   **c** catch

2 **Write the phrases from Exercise 1 in the correct place.**

1 _____ my sister
2 _____ the station
3 _____ the train

3 **Find and circle six verbs.**

I	N	V	I	T	E	G	E
M	A	H	M	B	J	E	N
A	P	T	P	R	K	M	J
G	Z	A	R	G	U	E	O
I	U	I	O	F	S	L	Y
N	D	Q	V	C	V	Y	N
E	P	R	E	D	I	C	T

__/18

Grammar

4 **Answer in sentences.**

```
MOUNT ROYAL HALL
BEYONCE TOUR
SEAT B15   7·30 P·M
NO PHOTOS!

          Kim Ballance
```

1 Where is Kim going this Saturday?
   _____

2 Where is Beyonce singing?
   _____

3 What time is the show starting?
   _____

4 Where is she sitting?
   _____

5 Is she taking a camera?
   _____

5 **Write two sentences about WonderCars 3000 from each box.**

1 [pollute Cars will be They electric won't]

a _____
b _____

2 [They be quieter Cars will won't fly.]

a _____
b _____

6 **Circle the correct word.**

1 WonderCars 3000 won't be noisy **and / but / because** they won't pollute the planet.
2 They won't be cheap **and / but / because** a lot of people will buy them.
3 I won't buy one **and / but / because** I haven't got any money.

__/16

Functions

7 **Order the words.**

1 Tom ice cream an afternoon for this you come like Would to ?
   _____

2 Mia, music I got lesson a Sorry, afraid I'm can't I've . .
   _____

3 Tom time OK, another maybe .
   _____

__/6

Your score   **Your total score**

__/40

31–40   21–30   0–20

22

3 Be Careful!

My Picture Dictionary

Injuries and illnesses

1 Write the words correctly.

1 irubse *bruise*
2 cmoatsh aehc
3 oerbnk egl
4 teib
5 locd
6 hootcahet
7 rsoe torhat
8 ahacere
9 unrb
10 raemertpuet
11 pirandes lekna
12 gucoh
13 hceeaadh
14 tcu

2 Circle the correct words.

1 Oh no! I can't sing today, I've got a **sore throat** / **broken leg**.
2 He fell on the glass and he's got a **burn** / **cut** on his hand.
3 Lily's face is red and she's very hot; she's got a **temperature** / **bruise**.
4 She jumped off the wall and now she's got a **bite** / **sprained ankle**.
5 I didn't wear my coat and now I've got a **stomach ache** / **cold**.
6 They ate the green fruit and then had **an earache** / **a stomach ache**.

3 Look at the words in Exercise 1. Underline the injuries.

my words

Do you know more words for illnesses and injuries? Write them here.

_____
_____
_____
_____

1 Read. Correct the underlined words in sentences 1-6 below.

Ocean Island Adventure

Try Something New!

Have you ever been for a long walk?

Of course you have!

But have you ever been for a walk under water?

This is your chance!

Call 902 300 600 502 for information

Mia Hey, Mum! Look at this!

Mum Oh dear, Mia. What about insect bites? And remember I got a stomach ache on holiday last year.

Mia Yes, and you got an earache on the plane too, and then you had a temperature and a cold ...

Mum Oh stop, Mia! I'm going to get a headache!

1 Mia is talking to her <u>dad</u>.
Mia is talking to her mum.
2 Ocean Island looks <u>boring.</u>

_____

3 Mia's mum is worried about <u>bruises.</u>

_____

4 She gets <u>a sore throat</u> on planes.

_____

5 She's going to get a <u>toothache</u> now.

_____

Talking Tips!

2 Match the sentences to the pictures.

I don't believe it.   It's no big deal.   Watch out!

Present perfect vs past simple

3 ⭐ Look at the table and answer true or false. Add two true sentences and two false ones.

	Never		Last week	
	Gina	Dave	Gina	Dave
win medal	✓			✓
be on TV		✓	✓	
break a leg	✓			✓
have an earache		✓	✓	
fall on the ice	✓			✓

1 Gina has never won a medal.   *true*
2 Gina broke her leg last week.
3 Dave has never fallen on the ice.
4 _____ (true)
5 _____ (false)
6 _____ (true)
7 _____ (false)

4 ⭐⭐ **Complete the table with the past simple or the past participle of the verbs.**

past simple	past participle
~~went~~	¹*gone*
²	seen
had	³
⁴	been
found	⁵
⁶	walked
was	⁷
⁸	hurt
won	⁹
¹⁰	fallen
broke	¹¹
¹²	made

5 ⭐⭐ **Read and complete with the underlined verbs from Exercise 4.**

Yesterday we ¹*went* to Ocean Island for a trip. We've never ²_____ there before. My grandma ³_____ a competition so she invited us. We went on an Underwater Walk. I've never ⁴_____ so many tropical fish before! The guides ⁵_____ some helmets and special shoes for us. You get cuts and bruises from the rocks and that can ⁶_____ . Have you ever ⁷_____ on the bottom of the sea? It's very difficult, but wonderful too. The water ⁸_____ cold and I ⁹_____ a sore throat in the evening. I always get sore throats on trips!
Here's a photo, cool hey?
Mo

6 ⭐⭐ **Order the words to make questions.**

1 Island before to Mo ever Has been Ocean ?
   Has Mo ever been to Ocean Island before?
2 did When go she ?
   _____
3 she What wear did ?
   _____
4 tropical Did see she fish ?
   _____
5 Has a had she sore throat ever ?
   _____
6 Was under to water it difficult walk ?
   _____

7 ⭐⭐⭐ **Answer the questions in Exercise 6.**

1 *Yes she has.*
2 _____
3 _____
4 _____
5 _____
6 _____

At the doctor's

8 **Separate the words in the dialogue.**

Doctor What'sthematter?What'swrong?
Fran   Myleghurts.I'vegotasorethroat.Myearhurts.
Doctor You'vebrokenit.Takethismedicine.
      Haveahotdrink.

9 **Write two dialogues. Use one phrase from each line in Exercise 8.**

1 Doctor _____
   Jim _____
   Doctor _____
2 Doctor _____
   Hannah _____
   Doctor _____

make, do and have

1 ⭐ Complete with *make, do* or *have.*

X-treme Weekend Camp

¹ *Have* fun!
² _____ friends.
³ _____ a new sport.
⁴ _____ sailing lessons.
Remember! ⁵ _____ your best
Be careful, and don't
⁶ _____ an accident!

Saturday
⁷ _____ your homework.
Don't ⁸ _____ mistakes!

Gemma!
⁹ _____ the dishes!
Don't ¹⁰ _____ a mess!

☺ I ¹¹ _____ an idea!

Sorry Mia, I ¹² _____ a stomach
ache today. Can you ¹³ _____
the shopping for the party? Can
you ¹⁴ _____ some sandwiches?
Thanks!
Lily.

How long? and for / since

2 ⭐ Read. Order the sentences (a–f).

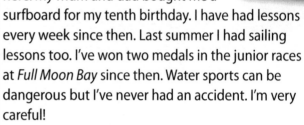

● ● ●

We have lived in Saratoga since I was nine. I'm fourteen now, and I love it here. My mum and dad bought me a surfboard for my tenth birthday. I have had lessons every week since then. Last summer I had sailing lessons too. I've won two medals in the junior races at *Full Moon Bay* since then. Water sports can be dangerous but I've never had an accident. I'm very careful!
Olivia

1 She won two medals.
2 She started surfing lessons.
3 Olivia came to live in Saratoga.   *a*
4 She had sailing lessons.
5 Her mum and dad bought her a surfboard.
6 She had her tenth birthday.

3 ⭐⭐ Write the words in the correct box.

last week ten minutes my birthday Saturday
an hour yesterday a month a long time 2020
four years half past three a few days she was nine
an evening

for	
since	last week

4 ⭐⭐ **Write the questions. Then answer with phrases from Exercise 3.**

1 how long / Olivia / live / Saratoga?
   How long has Olivia lived in Saratoga?

2 how long / Olivia / have / surfboard?
   _____
   _____

5 ⭐⭐ **Find the question and write the answer.**

Has Yes medal a has ever Olivia she won ?
_____ ?
_____ !

6 ⭐⭐ **Read about Tom and complete the questions and answers.**

Tom's Diary

Christmas 2009	1 February 2010	April 2010	5 July 2010	1 August 2010
Wow! I've got a new BMX bike! Lucky me!	My birthday! Hey! Dad's bought me a Kite!	Tennis Camp! Made friends with Joe, he's great!	Got new football. Cool!	TODAY!

1 Hi Tom, how long have you had your BMX bike?
   I've had it since *Christmas 2009.*
2 How _____ kite?
   _____ for _____
3 Hey! How _____ Joe?
   I've known _____ for _____
4 Hi! How _____ your football?
   _____ since _____

7 ⭐⭐ **Complete the paragraphs.**

Name:	Molly Black	Chris Drew	Joe Barry
Age:	15	13	12
Favourite Sport:	skateboarding	windsurfing	skydiving
Practised for:	one year	six months	one month
Competitions:	Interskate Games	Windy Kings Event	✗
Wins:	silver medal	✗	✗
Injury:	broken toe	sprained ankle	bruises

1 Joe is twelve. His favourite sport is _____ He hasn't been in any competitions and he hasn't won any medals. He's been practising for one month. Last week he fell into a tree, now he's got

   _____
2 Molly is _____
   _____
   Yesterday she dropped her skateboard, now _____
   _____
3 Chris _____
   _____
   On Saturday he fell into the water _____
   _____

8 ⭐ **Read. Complete the fact file for Luke.**

Name:	Luke Bond
Age:	
Favourite Sport:	
Practised for:	
Competitions:	
Wins:	
Injury:	

Luke Bond is fourteen. His favourite sports are surfing and diving. He has enjoyed water sports since he was five years old. He isn't very happy at the moment as he has had an accident. It isn't very serious. He fell off his mountain bike at the weekend. He was lucky, he's got a sprained ankle but there is nothing broken. He can't compete in the Water Wings Final this year. Last year he won the gold medal for the second time!

9 ⭐ **Answer the questions for Luke.**

1 Have you ever had an accident? *Yes, I have.*
2 Have you broken your leg?
3 How long have you been interested in your favourite sports?
4 Have you ever won a competition?

1 Order the words.

1 worried is Holly Dad about .
Holly is worried about Dad.

2 Max he's bored hungry and too is .
_____

3 tired her and hurt Holly's feet .
_____

4 amulet's scared shining The Holly and is .
_____

just / already / yet

2 ☆ True or false? In this picture:

1 Holly has just seen a crocodile.   *false*
2 Max hasn't hurt his leg yet.
3 They haven't found the amulet yet.
4 They haven't seen Nebi yet.
5 They've already looked by the pyramids.

3 ☆☆ Write a sentence about each person.

> Are we ready to go to the pyramid?

1 Nebi   Yes! / call / camel cab.

2 Akana   No! / not / pack / picnic.

3 Ra   Yes! / put on / magic amulet.

4 Shenti   No! / not / close / door.

1 Nebi *has just called the camel cab.*
2 Akana _____
3 Ra _____
4 Shenti _____

4 ☆☆☆ Complete the questions.

It was hot and Akana was bored. She didn't want to go to the market, or clean the boat. Her mother asked her to get some water from the river but she was tired. Akana put on her eye make up and then her jewellery. She loved her bracelets, they were beautiful. Yesterday she lost the shiny one but it was under the bed. Then she went for a walk with her friends.

> Akana! Have you ¹*been* to the market
> ² _____ ?

> Have you ³ _____ cleaned the boat?
> ⁴ _____ you got the water ⁵ _____ ?

> Have you ⁶ _____ done your make up?

> ⁷ _____ you ⁸ _____ your bracelet
> ⁹ _____ ?

5 ☆ **What is Nebi saying? Use the table to write sentences.**

I've	already	called climbed found seen cleaned	it

1   **Ra** She's calling the camel cab.
    Nebi _I've already called it._
2   **Ra** She's looking for the amulet.
    Nebi _____
3   **Ra** He wants to clean the boat.
    Nebi _____
4   **Ra** They're going to see the mummy.
    Nebi _____
5   **Ra** He's going to climb the pyramid.
    Nebi _____

6 ☆ **Where's the amulet? Complete with** _just_,
already **or** _yet_**. Then write your own dialogue.**

sarcophagus / pot
A Have you looked behind the sarcophagus ¹_yet_?
B I've ²_____ looked there now.
A Is it in the pot?
B No, I've ³_____ looked in the pot.

river / basket
A Have you looked in the river ⁴_____ ?
B I've ⁵_____ looked there now.
A Is it in the basket ?
B No, I've ⁶_____ looked in the basket.

Pharaoh's house / camel's bags
A _____
B _____
A _____
B _____

7 ☆ **Tick (✓) the activities you've done in column 1 and the activities you want to do in column 2.**

1	2
play football	go skydiving
play basketball	go hang gliding
sail a boat	climb a mountain
climb rocks	go skiing in Canada
go skating	run in a marathon
walk in the country	go surfing in Australia

8 ☆☆ **Write sentences about the activities in Exercise 7.**

1   _I've already walked in the country but I haven't run in a marathon yet._
2   _____
3   _____

Pharaoh's Fun
Find two words to complete the sentences.

Have ¹_____ seen Max? I think he's looking for ²_____ !

On the Edge has been a favourite TV programme since 1998. It started as a documentary about sports and it influenced young people who wanted to take risks and do their best. The programme has travelled around the world, and the presenters have interviewed surfing champions, Olympic medal winners, professional climbing teams and many other amazing people.

Edurne Pasaban, or 'Snowgirl', has climbed mountains since she was a child. She has won several prizes already and was the Spanish Champion Sportswoman of the year in 2005. Edurne has already climbed eleven mountains, all higher than 8,000 metres. She has just made plans to climb two more, Annapurna and Shisha Pangma. In 2004, aged thirty-one, Edurne climbed K2. It was a difficult climb and she had a bad injury. She was in hospital for months and lost two of her toes. But Edurne hasn't stopped yet, and she has never complained! She has just appeared on TV and talked about her experiences. She is not afraid to take risks and not afraid of injuries. Seth Coles, the presenter of the show, told the audience that it is important to have the correct medicines. Sore throats, headaches and sprained ankles can be a problem for new climbers. Climbing is a serious sport, and a risky one too!

Reading

1 Read the article. Find:

1 a TV show   *On the Edge*
2 two mountains
3 a sports champion
4 an injury
5 an illness

Writing

2 Imagine you are interviewing Edurne. Write five questions and answers.

You   How long have you climbed for?
Edurne ¹*Since I was a child.*
You   Have you ever ²_____ ?
Edurne ³_____
You   How many ⁴_____ ?
Edurne ⁵_____
You   How high ⁶_____ ?
Edurne ⁷_____
You   Have you ever ⁸_____ ?
Edurne ⁹_____

Time Detectives

My Picture Dictionary
Describing objects

1 Complete the words with the missing vowels.

1 m<u>e</u>t<u>a</u>l
2 sq_ _ r_
3 pl_st_c
4 g_ld
5 w_ _ d_n
6 _bl_ng

7 tr_ _ ng_l_r
8 d_ _ m_nd
9 gl_ss
10 r_ _nd
11 p_p_r
12 _v_l

2 Use the words in Exercise 1 to label the objects.

A _____
B _____
C _____
D _____
E _____
F _____
G _____
H _____
I _____
J _____
K _____
L _____

3 Circle the odd one out.

1 oval square (wooden) oblong
2 glass round plastic metal
3 paper triangular gold wooden
4 diamond glass metal oval

my words

Do you know more words for describing objects?
Write them here.

_____
_____
_____

1 Read and label the objects with words from the text.

Tom's class were visiting the Tate Modern, a famous art gallery in London. They had already seen a lot of different paintings and were tired. Some of the boys were complaining, and Tom wasn't listening. But there was one more room to see. It was a room full of rubbish! Rubbish? Now they were all listening! Mark Dion has collected rubbish from the River Thames for a long time. He has found all sorts of things, metal coins, glass bottles, plastic toys, shiny jewellery and big square chests made of wood. For Mark, these things are not rubbish but a part of the history of London and they tell us stories about people's lives.
The Tate Modern, has given him a room for the collection. Is it art? Is it treasure? Or is it rubbish? What do you think?

D _____

C _____

B _____

E _____

A *plastic toys*

2 Circle the correct word.

1 Tom's class were visiting the **River Thames /** **(Tate Modern.)**
2 They were **tired / bored**.
3 Mark Dion has collected **rubbish / paintings** for a long time.
4 He found all sorts of **objects / ghosts** in the river.
5 These things are now in a **room / a castle** in the Tate Modern.
6 The coins are made of **metal / glass**, and the toys are made of **plastic / gold**.

Talking Tips!

3 Find three words and use them to complete the dialogue.

(a h c w t) (h e n c i k c) (n d i w)

Bobby Oh no, there's a spider in my bag!
Amy What a ¹_____ ! It can't hurt you.
Bobby You know I hate spiders.
Amy Yes, oh look there's one behind your ear!
Bobby Don't ²_____ me up.
Amy It's true! He was just running down your neck, ³_____ out!

Past continuous

4 ☆ Complete with *was* or *were*.

Two girls ¹*were* looking for something on the beach.
They ²_____ digging in the sand.
The tall girl ³_____ smiling, but the small girl looked fed up.
Then they ⁴_____ both shouting!
One of the girls ⁵_____ holding a metal jewellery box.

5 ☆ Which ending do you prefer? Complete and then tick (✓) sentence a or b.

a That evening, they _____ wearing gold necklaces at a party.

or

b That afternoon, they _____ showing the metal jewellery box to the police.

6 What was in the metal jewellery box? Use the underlined letters in Exercise 4 to find out.

Gold necklaces and a _____ ring.

7 ⭐⭐ Rosie Parker was looking out of her window, watching the children. Write the questions and answers. Use the words in the box.

> yes / no he / she was / wasn't
> yes / no they were / weren't

1   girls / digging / beach ?
    Were the girls digging on the beach? Yes they were.

2   tall girl / smiling ?
    _____

3   small girl /smiling ?
    _____

4   one girl / holding / metal box ?
    _____

5   girls / wearing / jewellery / party ?
    _____

6   girls / showing / box / police ?
    _____

8 ⭐⭐ What were they doing on Saturday? Write sentences. Use the words in the box.

> ~~listen~~ have visit play watch dig

Saturday	
Mia	Egytian Art Museum ✓
Tom	BMX Championship ✗
Lily	Teen Rock Awards ✓
James	Interschools Tennis Match ✗
Class 5	Dig in Devon ✗
The football team	Picnic on River ✓

1   *Lily was listening to the Teen Rock Awards.*
2   Tom wasn't watching _____
3   Mia _____
4   James wasn't _____
4   Class 5 _____
6   The football team _____

Complaining

9 Write the words correctly.

I'm ¹*sick* (iskc) of museums and I'm
²_____ (oebrd) with history.
I'm ³____ (ridte) of sitting here and
I'm ⁴_____ (dfe pu) with working on
Sundays.

10 Match the sentences.

1   We were buying <u>shoes for school</u>. c
2   <u>The train</u> was an hour late and the children were complaining.
3   It was raining so there was no <u>football.</u>
4   Annie wasn't eating her <u>hamburger.</u>

a   They were <u>tired of</u> waiting.
b   She was <u>fed up with</u> fast food.
c   We were <u>bored with</u> shopping.
d   They were <u>sick of</u> watching TV.

11 ⭐⭐ Change the underlined words in Exercise 10 to make new sentences.

What was happening? How did they feel?

1   *We were buying clothes for a school trip. We were fed up with shopping.*

2   _____
    _____

3   _____
    _____

4   _____
    _____

1 Read. Order the sentences.

Charlotte was remembering a night in April 1912…

I was eating dinner with my family when I saw two men. They were wearing uniforms and walking quickly to the captain's table. I didn't hear anything while they were speaking but I watched the Captain's face. He was looking at them angrily and then they all left the dining room. Not long after that the captain came back into the dining room. He was holding some paper and his hand was shaking. He started speaking. He spoke fast but everyone was listening carefully to every word. The ship was sinking! It was sinking slowly and we had time, but not a lot of time! While the Captain was speaking a group of men got up noisily and shouted at him. They were running towards the door when the wall fell on top of them. I don't remember anything after that.

1   He spoke fast.
2   I was eating dinner.   *a*
3   They got up noisily.
4   His hand was shaking.
5   The wall fell on them.
6   He looked at them angrily.

Adverbs of manner

2 Complete the columns with words from the word search.

Q	U	I	C	K	L	Y	A
U	D	M	R	W	A	F	F
I	S	Y	T	L	M	D	X
E	C	A	R	E	F	U	L
T	I	G	H	F	E	Z	V
M	T	O	N	A	Q	U	Z
J	N	O	I	S	I	L	Y
B	O	D	C	T	K	G	P
J	A	N	G	R	I	L	Y

Adjectives	Adverbs
quick	¹ *quickly*
2 _____	quietly
angry	3 _____
4 _____	carefully
noisy	5 _____
6 _____	well
fast	7 _____

3 Find the correct ending for the sentence.

1   The men were shouting   noisily.

2   They left the dining room   angrily.

3   The captain followed them   fast.

4   They all moved   quietly.

5   Suddenly, water came in   quickly.

4 Complete the answers. Use the sentences in Exercise 3 to help you.

1 What were the men doing before they left the dining room?
They _were shouting angrily._

2 Who followed them?
The _____ them.

3 How did they all move?
_____ all _____

4 Was the Captain walking behind them noisily?
No, _____ . He was _____

5 What happened next?
The water _____ in _____

Past simple vs past continuous

5 ☆ Circle the correct words.

Charlotte ¹was running / ran to the boats when she ²was seeing / saw a man. While people ³were getting in / got in the boats, he ⁴ran / was running to the Captain's room and ⁵was hiding / hid behind the door. While he ⁶was hiding / hid, he ⁷was hearing / heard a noise and ⁸was running / ran. What ⁹was happening / happened to the treasure? He ¹⁰was dropping / dropped it . Years later some students ¹¹were swimming / swam in the sea when they ¹²were finding / found a wooden chest!

6 ☆ Read and answer the questions.

1 Was Carl Asplund taking his family to America?
Yes, he was.
2 Were they travelling by train?
3 Was Selma looking for treasure?
4 What happened on 14 April?
5 What were Selma's treasures?
6 When did she die?

Writing

7 ☆☆ Write your story in your notebook.
Choose A or B and add *then*, *after that* and *finally*.

	A	B
you are	a diver	an archaeologist
you were diving/digging when you saw	a small boat	a wooden chest
inside there was	money	jewellery
you examined it	carefully	slowly
you took it to	the police	a museum
criminals were looking for it, and for you	in Lima	in Santa Cruz
you were	scared!	in danger!
you were running	to the car	to the street
when a strange man	caught you	stopped you
you were arguing	noisily	angrily
you escaped from	the man	the criminal

The Titanic sank on 15 April 1912

First, Carl Asplund bought seven tickets for himself, his wife Selma, and his five children. They were going to start a new life in America. They were happy and excited.

Then, on 14 April *The Titanic* started to sink! There were people running everywhere. Some were lucky, but 1,500 people died in the tragedy. Someone pushed Selma Asplund into a small boat. Suddenly the little boat was in the water, but where was Carl? Selma never saw him again.

After that, a large ship *The Carpathia* took Selma to New York. Two of her children were with her. She had Carl's watch, some keys and his gold ring. These were Selma's treasures.

Finally, on 15 April 1964, exactly 52 years after the tragedy, Selma died. She was 91 years old.

The Magic Amulet

1 Read and complete then tick the correct picture.

~~hungry~~ dangerous snake basket tune music

This morning the sun was shining, again! I was feeling ¹_hungry_ and fed up. While we were talking to Ra we heard ²_____. A man was playing a ³_____. There was a round ⁴_____ next to him. It was moving slowly. We watched it for a moment and suddenly a ⁵_____ appeared. It was listening to the music and moving quietly. The snake was ⁶_____ but I wasn't bored anymore!

2 ⭐⭐ Order the words. Then, tick (✓) the sentences that are true.

1 was fed Max feeling up .
   Max was feeling fed up.

2 was raining It .
   _____

3 A was a tune playing man .
   _____

4 was to music dancing A snake .
   _____

5 noisily It moving was .
   _____

6 was with Max snake the bored .
   _____

used to

3 ⭐ Write true sentences.

Max and Holly The Egyptians	used to	eat pizza write hieroglyphs
	didn't use to	go to scribe school visit museums have amulets

1 _The Egyptians used to write hieroglyphs._
2 _____
3 _____
4 _____
5 _____

4 Use the underlined sentences to label the pictures.

I used to have a snake. <u>I used to keep it in the bathroom in a basket.</u> It didn't use to make a noise so nobody knew I had it. One day, my dad was having a shower when the snake came out. It didn't use to come out much. I was surprised and my dad was surprised too. He screamed. My poor snake was scared. It was hiding under the sink when I found it. It used to hide when it was scared. I gave it a rat to eat. <u>It used to like rats.</u> That day it wasn't hungry, or maybe it was sick of rats. I left it alone. The next day it wasn't there. <u>I don't know where it is now!</u>
Asim

a _____

b _____

c _____

5 Where is Asim's snake now? Write the sentence.

It'sonhishead!

_____

6 ★★ Complete the questions. Use *use to* and a verb from the box.

have live like come out do

1 What pet did you *use to have* ?
2 Where did the snake _____ ?
3 Did the snake _____ rats?
4 Did it _____ much?
5 What did it _____ when it was scared?

7 ★★ Complete Asim's answers.

1 I *used to have a snake.*
2 It _____
3 Yes, _____
4 No, _____
5 It _____

8 ★★★ Imagine you used to have a pet insect. Answer the questions.

1 What did you use to have?
  I used to have _____
2 Where did it use to live?

  _____
3 What did it use to eat?

  _____
4 What did it use to do?

  _____
5 Where is it now?

  _____

Let's Revise!

Vocabulary

1 Find the words and write them in the correct column.

> ob plas al tic o gular met er val
> en long re pap trian squa wood

Shapes

_____

_____

_____

_____

Materials

_____

_____

_____

_____

2 Complete.

Adjectives

1 _____   4angry

2 _____   5careful

3 _____

6 f_____

Adverbs

1quickly   4 _____

2noisily   5 _____

3quietly

___/21

Grammar

3 Complete with the past simple or the past continuous. Use these verbs.

> clean see listen wear look walk shout put sit hear

I ¹_____ on a bench by the river when I ²_____ something floating in the water. I picked it up and ³_____ at it. It was a metal sword in a plastic bag. Two girls ⁴_____ their dog nearby so I ⁵_____ to them. They didn't ⁶_____ me. They ⁷_____ to music. I ⁸_____ an old T shirt so I ⁹_____ the sword with it and ¹⁰_____ it in my bag carefully. Was it rubbish or treasure?

4 Molly used to live in Egypt. Write sentences about what she used to do.

climb pyramids ✓
have a pet crocodile ✗
sail down the Nile ✓
swim with snakes ✗
play the flute ✓

1 _____

2 _____

3 _____

4 _____

5 _____

___/10

Functions

5 Complete the sentences with two words from each box.

> with up of sick

1 I'm _____ watching TV!

> with tired up of

2 He's _____ reading this book.

> with up of bored

3 They're _____ computer games.

___/9

Your score   **Your total score**

___/40

😃 31–40   🙂 21–30   🙁 0–20

My Picture Dictionary

Describing jobs

1 Complete the words with the missing vowels and number the photos.

1 z<u>oo</u> ke<u>e</u>p<u>e</u>r
2 _ct_r
3 b_bys_tt_r
4 f_r_f_ght_r
5 sh_p _ss_st_nt
6 f_ct_ry w_rk_r
7 d_ct_r
8 p_l_t
9 ch__ff __r
10 v_t

2 Find the opposite adjectives in the word search.

1	dangerous	*safe*	4	exciting
2	challenging		5	varied
3	ordinary		6	badly-paid

R	E	P	E	T	I	T	I	V	E
I	A	W	O	R	K	V	E	R	Y
L	S	O	N	S	A	F	E	G	H
O	Y	D	U	R	S	A	N	D	I
W	E	U	A	R	A	U	N	I	F
O	G	L	A	M	O	R	O	U	S
W	E	L	L	P	A	I	D	R	M

3 Finish the sentence with the letters that are left in the word search.

I am a pilot and _____

4 Write sentences for these jobs.

1 I am a vet.

_____

2 I am a factory worker.

_____

my words

Do you know more adjectives for describing jobs?
Write them here.

_____

_____

_____

1 Read and answer.

Mandy's youth club are on a trip to Langly Safari Park.

Gill the driver Hello children. We are going to see a lot of different animals today, but we are not going to get too close. Please be careful, the animals are dangerous.

Mandy I know all about animals, my dad's a vet! He lets me help him sometimes. Hey! A lion!

Gill You're not allowed to shout here!

Mandy Sorry. Are we going to stop? I want to take a photo for my mum. She's a science teacher.

Gill That's interesting. There is a DVD of the park in the souvenir shop.

Mandy Great! I'll buy it.

1 Who drives people in the park?   *Gill the driver.*
2 Who works with animals?
3 Who works with children?
4 Who wants to take a photo?

2 What does Mandy want to be? Use the underlined letters in Exercise 1 to make the word.

Mandy wants to be a _____

Talking Tips!

3 Separate the words and complete the dialogue.

payattention(watchout)nowayhe'ssocute

Dad ¹*Watch out*, there's a lion and I think he's hungry!
Barny Oh, but ² _____ ! Will they let me touch him?
Dad ³ _____ ! Listen to the zoo keeper.
Barny Oh look! There's a zebra over there.
Dad Barny! Stand here and ⁴ _____ ! The man is saying something.

be allowed to / let / make

4 ☆☆ Order the words to make questions.

Langly Safari Park

Don't ...	But you can ...
stand up	have a drink
feed the animals	take photos
play music	have fun!
leave the bus	
touch the animals	

1 Are allowed photos we to take ?
   Are we allowed to take photos?
2 us Will let music you to listen ?
   _____
3 animals you us the Will let touch ?
   _____
4 to drink have allowed we a Are ?
   _____
5 the Are feed we animals to allowed ?
   _____
6 stand will let you us up ?
   _____
7 we Are allowed the bus to leave ?
   _____

5 ☆ Write the answers next to the questions in Exercise 4.

> No, sorry, it isn't allowed.   Yes, no problem.

6 ☆☆ Complete the sentences about Tom.

Questionnaire

My parents make me …	Tom	You
study.	✓	
tidy my room.	✓	
clean the car.	✗	
My parents let me …		
go out at weekends.	✓	
watch TV in my room.	✗	
go to bed late.	✗	
go on school trips.	✓	
take my MP3 player to school.	✗	

My parents make me ¹*study* and ² _____
They don't ³ _____
My parents ⁴ _____ and ⁵ _____
They ⁶ _____ or ⁷ _____ or ⁸ _____
_____

7 ☆☆☆ Now complete the questionnaire and write sentences that are true for you.

My parents make me _____
_____
_____
_____
_____
_____
_____

Apologising

8 Write the dialogues correctly.

1 Ididn'tmeannotobigIt'sscaredealyou

Alien	_____
Sam	_____

2 doesn'tiI'mItsorrymatter

Don	_____
Annie	_____

3 SorryitwasworryanaccidentDon't

Shark	_____
Matt	_____

9 Write dialogues for Mandy and Gill the driver.

1 Mandy is sitting on Gill's bag of crisps and now they are all broken.
Mandy   _____
Gill   _____

2 Mandy is eating a sandwich. It is Gill's lunch!
Mandy   _____
Gill   _____

5ᵇ First Jobs

1 Match the jobs with the pictures.

1 singer   *B*
2 cleaner
3 factory worker
4 waitress
5 teacher
6 chauffeur
7 secretary

2 Read and complete with the correct jobs from Exercise 1.

At first, life in the USA was hard and challenging. My dad, Guido, was a ¹*factory worker* and he was badly-paid. He was a ²t_____ before. My mum, Lola, worked in a café, but she wasn't a ³w_____ she was a ⁴c_____ . She worked long hours but she was happy because we were together. One day, she was singing in the café, when a man saw her. 'Can you act too?' he asked. That was the beginning! Now my mother is a famous ⁵s_____and her life is glamorous. She has a ⁶c_____ and a ⁷s_____ too. She works long hours. Is she happy? I don't know!

must / have to / should

3 ☆☆ Write sentences.

paperboy firefighter waitress shop assistant secretary	must have to should	be polite deliver papers be organised serve people wear a helmet

1   *A shop assistant has to serve people.*
2   _____
3   _____
4   _____
5   _____

4 ☆ Lily's class are going to Shakira's concert. They are staying in a hotel. What does Lily's mum say? Circle the correct words.

1 You **don't have to** / (**mustn't**) make a noise in the hotel.
2 You **mustn't** / **shouldn't** have your mobile on in the theatre.
3 You **don't have to** / **shouldn't** sing the songs with Shakira.
4 You **mustn't** / **don't have to** go to bed too late.
5 You **don't have to** / **shouldn't** buy the CD.
6 You **mustn't** / **shouldn't** forget your money.

5 ☆ Shakira's secretary, Maud, is interviewing a new chauffeur, Rob. Use the phrases below to complete the dialogue.

a No, you don't have to. Ned carries her things.
b No, Rob. You mustn't buy her presents and you mustn't take photos!
c Yes, you have to work on Saturdays, but not on Sundays.
d ~~You don't have to, but you should wear a white shirt, and you must wear a cap.~~
e Well, you have to be polite, of course.

Rob Must I wear a uniform?
Maud ¹*You don't have to, but you should wear a white shirt, and you must wear a cap.*
Rob Should I talk to Shakira?
Maud ²_____
Rob Do I have to carry her bags?
Maud ³_____
Rob Should I buy her flowers and chocolates?
Maud ⁴_____
Rob Must I work every weekend?
Maud ⁵_____

6 ☆☆ Complete the job adverts. You can use the words more than once.

use a computer speak English wear a uniform
be fit work quickly make phone calls

SECRETARY WANTED
Must _____
Should _____
Doesn't have to _____

PAPER BOY WANTED
Must _____
Should _____
Doesn't have to _____

7 ☆☆☆ Write the job adverts.

BABYSITTER WANTED
_____
_____
_____

_____WANTED
_____
_____
_____

Negative prefixes: *un, im, dis*

8 Write the word correctly next to the opposite word.

~~clkunyu~~ uytind sionedhts ynenuldrif meatintpi
faonbletucorm lebissiomp sigedsindaro

1 lucky *unlucky*
2 possible _____
3 patient _____
4 tidy _____
5 organised _____
6 honest _____
7 comfortable _____
8 friendly _____

9 Choose a babysitter, Mike or Sally?

Mike is friendly and honest but he is very untidy and impatient.

Sally is very organised and patient, and honest too. She is sometimes unfriendly.

I choose _____ because I think a babysitter should be _____
I don't think a babysitter has to be _____

The Magic Amulet

1 ⭐⭐ Order the words.

1 have find H<u>o</u>lly the and magic Max to amule<u>t</u> .
Holly and Max have to find the magic amulet.

2 rude mu<u>s</u>tn't <u>b</u>e to w<u>i</u>se the woman Max .
_____

3 find to chi<u>l</u>dren the have <u>s</u>phinx The .
_____

4 <u>m</u>ust take They care .
_____

5 now go They <u>s</u>hould .
_____

6 the f<u>i</u>nd clue have They to .
_____

2 Make a word from the underlined letters in Exercise 1 to finish the sentence.

It's _____ !

can / could

3 ⭐ Use the boxes to write questions and answers.

Can	you	speak English read hieroglyphs	now?
Could	he she	see into the future understand Egyptian	last year?

Yes,	I he	can / could.
No,	she	can't / couldn't.

1 *Could she see into the future last year? No, she couldn't.*

2 _____
3 _____
4 _____
5 _____

4 ⭐⭐ Write the questions. Use the words in the boxes.

Can teach you swim? you me? Could

Woman [1]*Can you swim?*
Max Yes, I can!
Woman [2]*Could you teach me?*

you Can hierolglyphs? show Could me? read you

Holly [3]_____
Woman Of course!
Holly [4]_____

you Can computer? teach a Could me? use you

Ra [5]_____
Max Yes, it's easy!
Ra [6]_____

show Could the me? you you Can break code?

Holly [7]_____
Nebi Yes, I can.
Holly [8]_____

5 ⭐⭐⭐ **Write Holly and Max's questions.**

Max and Holly are excited. They find a tomb and they can see a door. Holly wants to go in. She asks Ra. There's an old statue inside. Max wants to touch it. Ra doesn't allow him to touch it, but Holly sees some Egyptian hieroglyphs on it. She wants Ra to read it. She doesn't understand, but Ra can explain. Max is tired and wants to go back. He is hungry too and he asks Ra for some food.

Holly:
1 *Can we go in?*
2 _____
3 _____

Max:
4 _____
5 _____
6 _____

6 ⭐ **Nebi found an amulet. Match the sentences.**

1 The amulet
2 Now I can
3 I couldn't
4 Could you
5 Can I

a see inside?
b can help me.
c take me to the pyramid.
d read hieroglyphs before.
e break codes!

7 ⭐⭐⭐ **You found an amulet! Answer the questions then draw your amulet.**

What can it do? _____
What couldn't you do before? _____
Write a question for the amulet. _____

Pharaoh's Fun
Find two words in the picture. Use the words to complete the sentences.

Do you want to ¹ _____ more about Egypt?
Ra can ² _____ you!

Teach
Learn

Top Jobs

Reading

1 Read. Correct the sentences below.

Hello, I'm Benson. My job is great. I look after animals, but I'm not a zoo-keeper and I'm not a vet. I work at an elephant centre in Nairobi. Our elephants come from all over Africa, and some have serious injuries. Many of them are very weak and hungry at first. Their mothers are dead. We have to give the babies milk from bottles, and sleep with them at night time. Sometimes they are scared and unhappy. We work very long hours and we all wear green uniforms. Every day we play with them and look after them, so they know us. We help them to get well. Our days are never dull!

Every morning the public are allowed to come and visit the centre. They mustn't come too close, and we don't let them give the elephants food. They are allowed to watch an elephant football game and take photos. They shouldn't touch the elephants. They can ask a lot of questions and we are happy to answer. There is more information on our website: http://www.sheldrickwildlifetrust.org/

The elephants don't have to go back to the wild until they are ready. We have to be very careful and patient too. The elephants need time to learn to live a different life. My job is very challenging and varied. It isn't very well-paid but I'm lucky, I love it! It's very exciting to work with these beautiful animals and to help them live in the wild again. When they go, we never forget them, and they remember us too because elephants never forget!

Writing

2 You are at the elephant centre. Write a postcard to a friend.

Dear _____
I am at the _____ today.
It's amazing. We are allowed
to _____
_____
but we mustn't _____
_____
_____
_____
_____
From _____

1 Benson works with computers. *Benson works with elephants.*
2 He wears a blue cap.
3 The public are allowed to visit in the afternoons.
4 When they are ready the elephants go to the zoo.
5 Benson's job is very dull and repetitive.

My Picture Dictionary

Describing clothes

1 Use one word from each circle to label the clothes in the picture. You can use the words more than once.

baggy
spotty
short
smart ~~floral~~
plain stripy
checked

jacket
jeans
trousers
~~scarf~~ skirt
T-shirt
jumper

1 *floral scarf*
2 _____
3 _____
4 _____
5 _____
6 _____
7 _____
8 _____

2 Circle the odd one out.

1 long (jacket) tight unusual
2 jumper fashionable jeans skirt
3 casual baggy trousers old fashioned

3 Complete.

I think the baggy jeans are interesting but the _____ is boring!
I think the _____ is _____ and the _____

my words

Do you know more for describing clothes?
Write them here.

_____
_____
_____

Record Breakers

1 **Read. Order the pictures (1-6).**

At first, jeans were not very fashionable but they were comfortable. Men wore them for work in factories, mines and on farms. They were plain blue, not very smart and the legs were not very tight. By 1940, the legs were shorter and tighter. Later, in the 1950s, they were the uniform of rock 'n' roll stars and their fans. Elvis Presley always wore tight jeans.

In the 1960s, jeans changed again. They became more colourful. Some had floral patterns and wide legs were fashionable. They were fantastic! Thirty years later, it was old-fashioned to wear jeans painted with flowers, everybody was wearing jeans with holes in them and bright, coloured jeans were popular too. Levi's were popular but more expensive than other jeans.

What about today? Now, we wear baggy, comfortable jeans with long legs and big pockets, or smart jeans with straight legs. All jeans are fashionable!

Have you got a pair?

2 **True or false?**

1 Elvis wore baggy jeans. *false*
2 Factory workers wore comfortable jeans.
3 Jeans with floral patterns were old-fashioned in the 1990s.
4 Jeans have to be blue.
5 In 1950 jeans were the school uniform in England.
6 Levi's were popular but expensive twenty years ago.

3 **Draw and describe a pair of jeans.**

_____
_____
_____
_____
_____

4 **Separate the words to find a sentence.**

Americansspendfourteenbilliondollarsayearonjeans!

_____

comparatives / superlatives

5 ☆ **Complete the table.**

adjective	comparative	superlative
¹*long*	² _____	the longest
³ _____	heavier	⁴ _____
tight	⁵ _____	⁶ _____
⁷ _____	⁸ _____	the most colourful
expensive	⁹ _____	¹⁰ _____
¹¹ _____	more comfortable	¹² _____
good	¹³ _____	¹⁴ _____

6 ⭐⭐ **Complete the sentences about the jeans in Exercise 1.**

| ~~longer~~ best tighter more fashionable |
| most expensive baggiest more comfortable |

1 The jeans in picture A have got *longer* legs than the jeans in picture B.
2 Elvis's jeans are _____ than the jeans in picture E.
3 The jeans in D are _____ than the jeans in picture B.
4 The most modern jeans are the _____
5 Levi's are the _____ jeans.
6 Wider legs were _____ in the 1960's than they are now.
7 Which jeans do you like _____?

7 ⭐ **Use the sentences below to complete the dialogue.**

a Thanks! Great!
b No, these are baggier than the expensive ones. I've got another pair.
c Well not the best ones, I want the older jeans.
d ~~I'm looking for my old jeans.~~

Mia Hi! What are you doing Lily?
Lily ¹*I'm looking for my old jeans.*
Mia Which jeans? You've got lots!
Lily ² _____
Mia I know, look here they are!
Lily ³ _____
Mia Well here are your most expensive ones!
Lily ⁴ _____
Mia What are going to do with them?
Lily Mia, did you know that jeans can help build houses? There's a website about it. I'm going to give them these jeans. They don't really fit me anymore.
Mia What a cool idea!

http://kids.nationalgeographic.com/Stories/
MoreStories/Guinness-clothes

8 ⭐⭐⭐ **Answer the questions about the dialogue in Exercise 7.**

1 Is Lily giving away her baggiest jeans?
   No, she's giving away her oldest jeans.
2 Are the baggiest jeans the most expensive?
   _____
3 Are the older jeans the best ones?
   _____
4 Has Lily got a lot of jeans?
   _____
5 Do the expensive jeans fit her?
   _____
6 What can people do with jeans?
   _____

9 **What's inside each drawer? Write sentences.**

smart stripy yellow new shirt
scarf long pink old spotty
baggy green T-shirt checked
casual skirt plain black
blue fashionable jeans new
floral jacket old casual

1 *A new, smart, stripy, yellow shirt.*
2 _____
3 _____
4 _____
5 _____
6 _____

1 Read and circle the correct words.

The Best Party in Town!
Mia's house, Saturday at 6 p.m.
Clothes should be casual.
Must be stripy, spotty or both!

Tom Hi Lily, I'm looking for something to wear to Mia's ¹**party** / **show**. Have you got any ideas?

Lily Well it has to be ²**stripy** / **colourful** or ³**floral** / **spotty**.

Tom I know! I've got my smart ⁴**stripy** / **checked** shirt.

Lily Oh no, Tom! You should wear something ⁵**baggier** / **more casual**.

Tom Do you think it's too ⁶**old-fashioned** / **smart**? It's very ⁷**plain** / **fashionable**!

2 Answer the questions about Exercise 1.

1 Where are Tom and Lily going on Saturday?
   They are going to Mia's party.

2 What is Tom looking for?
   _____

3 What does he want to wear?
   _____

4 Does Lily agree?
   _____

5 Describe Tom's shirt.
   _____

6 Why does Tom like it?
   _____

Talking Tips!

3 Complete the dialogue with the words in the box.

~~you~~ on up don't ready
wind in what's hang rush up

Tina Are ¹*you* ²_____ , Viv?

Viv ³_____ ⁴_____ , I can't find my jeans.

Tina Hurry up, Viv!

Viv Why ⁵_____ ⁶_____ ?

Tina Mum's ⁷_____ a ⁸_____ .

Viv Oh ⁹_____ ¹⁰_____ me ¹¹_____ , there's lots of time.

(not) as … as / less / the least

4 ⭐⭐ Order the words.

1 best fit friend as not as my I'm .
   I'm not as fit as my best friend.

2 My is best teacher as our friend as tall .
   _____

3 uniform My are clothes less a boring school than .
   _____

4 My isn't best as my friend as sporty brother/sister .
   _____

5 friend's My is bag as bag my heavy as .
   _____

6 David Beckham than famous I'm less .
   _____

5 ⭐⭐⭐ Compare the party hats and complete the sentences.

	Mia's	Lily's	Tom's
price	£5	£1	50p
glamorous	⭐⭐⭐	⭐⭐	⭐⭐⭐⭐⭐
tall	⭐⭐	⭐⭐⭐⭐⭐	⭐⭐⭐
smart	⭐⭐⭐⭐⭐	⭐⭐	⭐⭐⭐

1 Tom's hat is the least _expensive_.
2 Lily's _____ the least _____
3 Mia's hat is not as _____
4 _____
5 Which do you think is the least interesting? _____
6 Which is the least comfortable? _____

6 ⭐⭐ **Write sentences about Tom's and Zak's party trousers.**

Tom   **Zak**

Tom's trousers Zak's trousers	are aren't	as less	baggy unusual smart casual expensive glamorous	as less	than	Zak's trousers Tom's trousers

1 _Tom's trousers are as expensive as Zak's trousers._
2 _____
3 _____
4 _____
5 _____
6 _____

7 ⭐⭐⭐ **Read the sentences in Exercise 4. Tick (✓) the ones that are true for you. Add two true and two false sentences.**

1 _____
2 _____
3 _____
4 _____

Fashion verbs

8 **Write the words correctly.**

1 tfi
fit

2 gtnriy no
_____

3 ogoklni orf
_____

4 srsde pu
_____

5 utis
_____

6 og ihwh
_____

9 **Complete the text with words from Exercise 8.**

Lily is ¹_looking for_ some spotty or stripy clothes. She doesn't like to ²_____ for parties. Stripes don't ³_____ her so she is ⁴_____ _____ a spotty skirt. The colours don't ⁵_____ _____ her hair. The skirt doesn't ⁶_____ her very well but it's cheap. Should she buy it?

10 ⭐⭐⭐ **Change the shaded words in Exercise 9 to make a paragraph about James.**

James is looking for _____
_____
_____
_____
_____

The Magic Amulet

1 Complete the text.

shop wig amulet help uncomfortable message fit souvenir picture read

Max and Holly are in a souvenir ¹shop. Max is wearing a ²_____. It doesn't ³_____ and it's ⁴_____. He can't see. He breaks a ⁵_____ The picture is the best ⁶_____ in the shop and the man is very angry. Holly sees a picture of the ⁷_____ and thinks there is a ⁸_____ on the stone. She can't ⁹_____ it. Ra thinks that Nebi can ¹⁰_____ and they go to the palace school. Can Nebi help? Wait and see!

look / look like

2 ⭐⭐ Complete column three with the correct words.

a statue they've lost their money tired a film star worried the shoes are too tight interesting old hungry there's a message on the wall

You He / She / It They	look / looks look like / looks like	adjectives 1 _____ 2 _____ 3 _____ 4 _____ 5 _____ nouns ⁶a statue. 7 _____ sentences 8 _____ 9 _____ 10 _____

3 ⭐ Use the table in Exercise 2 to write sentences.

1 *He looks like a statue!*
2 _____
3 _____
4 _____
5 _____
6 _____

4 ⭐ Look at the picture in Exercise 1 and circle the correct words.

1 The man **looks** / **looks like** angry.
2 Max **looks like** / **looks** an Egyptian.
3 They don't **look** / **look like** they are happy.
4 The shop **looks like** / **looks** interesting.
5 It **looks like** / **looks** there's an amulet in the picture.
6 The wig doesn't **look** / **look like** comfortable.

CANDLES

5 ⭐⭐⭐ **Look at the candles in the picture and write sentences about them.**

1   *It looks like an Egyptian pyramid!*
2   _____ expensive!
3   _____
4   _____
5   _____ interesting!

Shopping for clothes

6 **Separate the words to make sentences about shopping.**

1   Excuseme,I'mlookingforafashionablejacket.
    Excuse me, I'm looking for a fashionable jacket.

2   Wherearethechangingroomsplease?
    _____

3   Whatsizeareyou?
    _____

4   Doesitfityou?
    _____

5   It'stootight.Haveyougotabiggerone?
    _____

6   I'masize10.
    _____

7   They'reoverhere.
    _____

8   Here'sacheckedone.
    _____

7 **Complete the dialogue in the correct order with the sentences from Exercise 6.**

Customer ¹*Excuse me, I'm looking for a fashionable jacket.*
Shop Assistant ² _____
Customer ³ _____
Shop Assistant ⁴ _____
Customer ⁵ _____
Shop Assistant ⁶ _____
A few minutes later ...
Shop Assistant ⁷ _____
Customer ⁸ _____

8 **Write your own dialogue. You are a looking for some trousers. You are a size 12. You want plain, blue jeans but the ones you try on are too baggy. You really want some that are smarter!**

_____
_____
_____
_____
_____
_____
_____

6ᵈ Let's Revise!

Vocabulary

1 Find ten words for describing clothes in the wordsearch. Circle the style adjectives in red and the pattern adjectives in blue.

F	A	S	H	I	O	N	A	B	L	E
B	C	P	C	D	E	S	M	A	R	T
G	A	O	H	M	L	T	P	G	S	I
Q	S	T	R	I	P	Y	W	G	Y	G
F	U	T	A	D	N	K	P	Y	Z	H
V	A	Y	C	H	E	C	K	E	D	T
F	L	O	R	A	L	O	U	X	P	E
C	O	L	O	U	R	F	U	L	J	R

2 Circle the correct verb.

1 He doesn't like **dressing up / looking for** new clothes.
2 The shirt doesn't **fit / go with** his eyes.
3 The girls are **trying on / dressing up** party clothes.
4 The yellow football shirts **don't suit / dress up** the players.

___/14

Grammar

3 Complete the sentences using the comparative or superlative of the adjective in brackets.

1 David Beckham is the _____ (famous) footballer in the world.
2 I think he is probably the _____ (well-paid) too!
3 His life is _____ (glamorous) than my life.
4 I think he's _____ (smart) than some footballers.

4 Complete the dialogue with *less* or *least*.

Mia Look at that jacket. It's the ¹_____ expensive in the shop.
Lily Yes, it's ²_____ expensive than the spotty on.
Mia You're right. It's also the ³_____ fashionable.
Lily It looks ⁴_____ comfortable than the spotty one too.
Mia Let's try on the spotty one!

5 Complete the sentences with *look / look like / looks / looks like*.

1 They don't _____ a happy family.
2 Dad _____ worried.
3 Mum _____ an Egyptian mummy.
4 The children _____ bored.

6 Order the words.

1 Lily well as Britney as sing can .
_____
2 glamorous Britney's Her is as costume as costume .
_____
3 famous She as isn't Britney as .
_____

___/16

Functions

7 Find two questions

it Does What size you are fit you
1 _____?
2 _____?

8 Find two answers.

12 it size No I'm doesn't
1 _____!
2 _____!

9 Now match the questions and answers from Exercise 6 and 7.

1 _____ ? _____ !
2 _____ ? _____ !

___/10

Your score	Your total score
	___/40
😀 31–40	🙂 21–30	☹ 0–20

54

My Picture Dictionary

Communication

1 Match the phrases.

1	tell	a	a dream
2	have	b	a story
3	send	c	the truth
4	make up	d	a message
5	tell	e	an argument
6	make	f	a joke
7	keep	g	a secret
8	make	h	a phone call
9	tell	i	a lie
10	have	j	an excuse

2 Label the pictures with the phrases from Exercise 1.

3 Separate the words to make sentences. Tick the sentences that are true for you.

1 Imakeaphonecalleveryday

_____

2 Mybestfriendcan'tkeepasecret

_____

Write two more true sentences.

3 _____

4 _____

Do you know more communication words? Write them here.

_____

_____

_____

1 Complete the dialogue.

Lily What are you doing Tom?

Tom [1]*I'm sending a message to Zak. We're going to see the new James Bond film today. Do you want to come?*

Lily I can't I'm going to see my aunt, the one who lives in Australia.

Tom [2]_____

Lily Oh, Tom, don't wind me up! She's here on holiday.

Tom [3]_____

Lily Tom! I don't tell lies! Well ... not very often!

Tom [4]_____

Lily You don't have to; James Bond films are all the same. It'll be about a beautiful girl who is really a spy.

a Can't you make an excuse? You can say you are going to the dentist.

b Don't worry, I'll tell you the story tomorrow.

c ~~I'm sending a message to Zak. We're going to see the new James Bond film today. Do you want to come?~~

d No way! Are you going to Australia then?

2 Circle the correct answer.

1 Tom's (sending a message to)/ having an **argument with** Zak.

2 Lily's **going to Australia / visiting her aunt** today.

3 Tom wants her to **keep a secret / make an excuse**.

4 Lily **always / usually** tells the truth.

5 Tom's going to tell her **the story / a joke** tomorrow.

6 James Bond films are all **dreams / the same**.

Talking Tips!

3 Match the phrases.

1 Have you seen Sophie's new puppy?   c

2 Oh no, there's our new sports teacher.

3 My cat is scared of mice!

4 What's in your bag?

a Don't be nosey!

b Quick, hide!

c ~~He's so cute!~~

d What a chicken!

Relative pronouns and clauses

4 ☆ Write five sentences.

a good looking man a beautiful girl a bad man a car an unusual place a machine a country	who that which where	goes too fast is far away wants to kill the spy loves the spy works as a spy there is secret information breaks codes

In James Bond films there is often ...

1 *a good looking man who works as a spy.*

2 _____

3 _____

4 _____

5 _____

6 _____

5 ☆ Circle the correct answer. Choose a sentence to label the photo.

1 Mma Ramotswe is a large lady detective (who)/ **where** comes from Botswana.

2 Botswana is a country **that / where** is close to Zambia, in Africa.

3 African tea grows in the mountains **who / which** are near the town.

4 Grace Makutsi is a secretary **who / which** came to work with Mma Ramotswe.

5 They both help people **where / who** have problems.

6 Mma Ramotswe drives a small white van **that / who** she loves.

6 ⭐⭐ **Order the words.**

1 travels who the I'm world English spy an .
I'm an English spy who travels the world.

2 that a fast I've got white doesn't go van very .
_____

3 films I'm are in lot a which of famous .
_____

4 My office in husband garage works next a that is to my .
_____

5 I problems in trouble solve who are for people .
_____

6 a is I of information lot that top secret have .
_____

7 Africa I which country in Botswana, is a in live .
_____

8 adventures have I countries where go to different I .
_____

7 ⭐ **Who are the sentences about? Write the numbers from Exercise 6 in the correct column.**

James Bond	Mma Ramotswe
1	

8 ⭐ **Match the sentences.**

1 My favourite Mma Ramotswe story is about the footballers.   *d*
2 Mma Ramotswe went to the stadium
3 She talked to the players
4 Her son saw the players were wearing tight shoes
5 He told Mr. Molofololo
6 Mr Molofololo bought trainers

a which were the right size for every player.
b where they played.
c who owned the team.
d ~~who lost the match.~~
e that didn't fit them.
f who were in the team.

Mma Ramotswe and her son solved the mystery, so the footballers could win again!

9 ⭐⭐ **Complete the paragraph about the film.**

~~a spy~~ can't keep a secret a key   disappears
the phone rings

This is the film that is about
¹ *a spy* who ²_____
There's a ³_____ that
⁴_____

There's a haunted train where
⁵_____ all the time.
It's really scary!

Body Language

1 Read and answer.

We all use body language, even animals! Have you got a pet? A cat or a dog?

I've got both. My cat, DJ, closes his eyes and shakes when he hears a loud a noise. That means he isn't happy! When he is cross he shows me all his teeth, and makes a noise like a snake.

Rambo, my dog, can communicate very well and I always know what he wants. He stands up on his back legs and puts his head on my knees when he is tired. When he's hungry he pushes his bowl across the kitchen with his nose.

Rambo is always the first to know that Dad's coming home. He runs down the stairs and puts his head to one side. His ears go up and he sits very quietly and waits. That is the sign that the car is coming down the street in a few minutes. How does he know? It's a mystery!

Lily

1 What does DJ do when he is cross? *He shows Lily all his teeth, and makes a noise like a snake.*
2 What does Rambo do when he is hungry?
3 What does he do when he is tired?
4 How does Lily know that DJ isn't happy?
5 Look at the picture of Rambo.
 What does this mean?

Body language

2 Find fourteen words in the word search. Circle the verbs in red and the parts of the body in blue. Which word appears twice?

E	Y	E	B	R	O	W	S	C
Y	A	P	L	A	Y	L	H	M
E	H	F	S	I	H	E	A	D
S	A	R	M	S	V	G	K	F
B	I	T	L	E	G	S	E	O
Z	R	N	O	S	E	G	U	L
Q	C	R	O	S	S	W	N	D
Y	R	D	K	T	O	U	C	H

3 Use words from the word search to label each picture.

1 *shake* your *head*
2 _____ your _____
3 _____ your _____
4 _____ your _____
5 _____ your _____
6 _____ with your _____
7 _____ into my _____

4 Complete with words from Exercise 3. Tick the ones that are true for you.

1 I *shake* my h*ead* when I am disappointed.

2 I p_____ with my h_____ when I am nervous.

3 I f_____ my a_____ when I am annoyed.

4 I r_____ my e_____ when I am surprised.

5 I l_____ into people's e_____ when I am telling the truth.

6 I c_____ my l_____ when I am tired.

7 I t_____ my n_____ when I am telling a lie.

may / might

5 ☆ Match the sentences.

1 They're playing with their hair. c
2 He's touching his nose!
3 He's raising his eyebrows.
4 She's folding her arms.
5 She's shaking her head.
6 She's crossing her legs.

a She might be angry!
b I think she may be disappointed.
c I think they might be embarrassed.
d He might be surprised.
e He may be telling a lie.
f She might be hiding something.

6 ☆ Tom and Zak are waiting for Mia. Find the second line to each verse of the chant.

She may have missed the early train,
[1] *She may have won a trip to Spain.*
She might not know it's after nine!
[2] _____

She might not want to come at all,
[3] _____

She may have cut her hand or head
[4] _____

Do you want to wait with me?
[5] _____

a She may be sleeping in her bed.
b She may have won a trip to Spain.
c She might not know there isn't time,
d She might not come, we'll have to see.
e She may be out with John or Paul.

7 ☆☆ Order the dialogue.

Tom Why do you think that?
Zak She's shaking her head, and now she's shouting too!
Zak I think she might be feeling cross.
Tom Look there's Mia!   1

8 ☆☆☆ Change the underlined words in Exercise 7 and write another dialogue.

Lily _____
James _____
Lily _____
James _____

9 ☆☆☆ Complete the sentences with your own ideas.

1 Your friend is talking to her teacher and shaking her head.
   She might be feeling _____

2 You friend is wearing a hat and two scarves.
   He might _____

3 Your friends are celebrating today.
   They _____

1 Change the underlined words to correct the text. Use the words in the box.

~~the school~~ boys a wig clue obelisk help
horse and chariot wait surprised

the school
This must be ¹the supermarket where Nebi works.
There are some ²girls from his class. Holly, you have
to ³go in. I will give you ⁴a hat to wear. Nebi will be
⁵disappointed to see you. Tell him that we have found
the ⁶amulet. He may ⁷annoy you. Then we might take a
⁸camel train and go to the ⁹pyramid. He can't follow us.

a _____ b _____

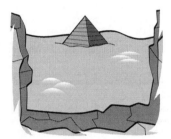
c _____ d _____

2 Answer the questions.

1 Where does Nebi work? *the school*
2 What is Holly wearing?
3 How does Nebi feel when he sees her?
4 What have the children found?
5 Where might they go?
6 How might they go to the obelisk?

must / can't

3 Write sentences for each picture.

This It We	must can't	be	in Egypt! the pyramid! a wig! the sphinx!

4 ⭐⭐ Order the words.

Ra it This be Nebi's I'm school! right, must is!
_____

Nebi Holly What Max! It and can't surprise! be a
_____

5 ⭐ Complete with *must* or *can't*.

1 He's got his arms folded. He *must* be angry.
2 They aren't laughing, he _____ be telling a joke.
3 She's raising her eyebrows. She _____ be surprised.
4 They're shouting. They _____ be having an argument.
5 He looks nervous. He _____ be telling the truth.
6 They're playing happily. They _____ be scared.

6 Follow the clues to find the word that finishes the sentence.

1 The first letter is also the first letter of this sentence.
2 The fourth letter is the second letter of the fourth month of the year.
3 The second and last letter are the same.
4 Holly's brother's name starts with the third letter.
5 The fifth letter is the ending of 'camel'.
6 The last letter is in leg, twice in eyes, but not in arms.

THE OBELISK IS AT THE

_____

Making deductions

7 ⭐⭐ Order the words to make sentences about the photo. Tick (✓) the sentence you agree with.

1 can't It be a that's cup, impossible !
2 drawing I'm it's sure a .
3 it isn't certain that I'm real .
4 a cup It be must !

8 Separate the words and complete the phrases.

mustcertainimpossible

1 I'm _____ it's moving!
2 It _____ be moving!
3 No, that's _____!

Pharaoh's Fun

Look at the picture below. Complete with the phrases from Exercise 8.

Tom thinks that it is moving.

_____

Mia thinks it can't be moving.

Lily thinks it is moving but doesn't believe it!

_____

What do you think?

Secret Messages

Reading

1 **Read. Match the sentences below.**

N'kisi is Aimee Morgana's African Grey parrot. He doesn't use sign language, he speaks! N'kisi is a parrot that can use and understand more than 900 words. He likes telling Aimee how he is feeling and what he is thinking. He might tell you that he is feeling annoyed or nervous, or he may talk about what he is doing. He uses sentences, and his grammar is very good!

Aimee talked to Dr. Sheldrake about N'kisi. Dr. Sheldrake is a scientist who looks at how animals communicate. They decided to try an experiment with N'kisi. They put different pictures in envelopes. They were pictures that N'kisi didn't see before the experiment. Aimee went to another part of the house and slowly opened the envelopes. She didn't speak. She just looked at the pictures and thought about them. N'kisi, who was in another room, said words and sentences connected to the pictures. One picture was of a driver in a car with his head out of the window. When Aimee looked at that picture, N'kisi said *Oh, careful! You put your head out!* How did N'kisi know that Aimee was looking at that picture? Some people say it must be a trick or a joke. Other people are certain that it is true.

What do you think? Is it possible that N'kisi can read Aimee's thoughts? Aimee is sure that the answer is YES!

1 Aimee is the woman *b*
2 N'kisi is the parrot
3 Dr. Sheldrake is a scientist
4 The pictures

a which they used were all different.
b ~~who has a grey parrot.~~
c that can read thoughts.
d who looks at different animals.

Writing

2 **Finish the sentences.**

1 Aimee is sure that *N'kisi can read her thoughts.*
2 N'kisi might _____
3 A lot of people raise their _____
  when they hear about N'kisi.
4 They think it can't _____!

3 **Answer for Aimee.**

Tell me three things about your amazing parrot.

_____
_____
_____

What do people say to you about N'kisi?

_____
_____
_____

8 Our World

My Picture Dictionary

Things on the beach

1 Circle the words and match with the pictures (1-16).

14
seagullfishingboattincancrisppacketjellyfish

beachumbrellawaterbottleturtleseaweedshell

cardboardboxsweetwrapperrock

sandrubbishbinplasticbag

2 Add one more to each set. Which group should not be on the beach?

a   sweet wrapper   tin can   plastic bag   _____

b   seagull   jellyfish   _____

c   rock   sand   _____

d   beach umbrella   rubbish bin   _____

Do You Care?

1 Read and find Tom and Mia's answer. Use the letters that are underlined to make the words.

Tom Hey, let's have lunch at the beach today.

Mia Great, how about a barbecue?

Tom No, we can't do that. If it's hot, they put fire danger signs everywhere.

Mia How about a picnic? We can take the beach umbrella.

Tom No, I was thinking about the café. There's too much rubbish on the beach, and I always get sand in my sandwiches.

Mia Oh, Tom! You are funny! But you are right; if there are tin cans and plastic bags on the rocks, it's no fun to be there.

Tom I think we should help to clean it up.

Mia Mmm, let's talk to the others and organise something.

Tom's Mum Hey, you two, we're going to eat at *The Fisherman's Boat Restaurant*. Do you want to come with us?

Tom and Mia y____ _____ !

2 Circle the correct answer.

1 A barbecue is a bad idea because it **isn't hot today** / **might be dangerous.**

2 Tom doesn't like picnics because he gets sand in his **shoes / sandwiches.**

3 There is a lot of rubbish **on the beach / in the café.**

4 The children want to **help clean it up / sit under the beach umbrella.**

5 They are going to eat **at home / in a restaurant.**

The environment

3 Find four verbs and five nouns in the word search.

W	A	T	E	R	H	L
D	R	O	P	E	E	I
L	U	P	E	C	N	G
V	B	I	R	Y	R	H
O	B	N	M	C	E	T
F	I	R	E	L	U	S
E	S	A	V	E	S	N
T	H	P	A	P	E	R

Complete the sentence with the letters that are left in the word search.

Please _____ the _____ !

4 Complete the sentences with words from the word search.

1 Do you always switch off the l*ights*?

2 I hope you r_____ your p_____!

3 Remember to put out the f_____!

4 We always s_____ the w_____.

5 Please pick up your r_____!

6 Everybody must r_____ their plastic bags.

7 Don't d_____ the glass! It's dangerous!

5 Circle the correct answer.

1 **Pick up** / **light** the plastic bag.

2 **Drop / save** water.

3 **Reuse / put out** paper.

4 **Recycle / switch off** the lights.

5 Pick up **lights / rubbish.**

6 Light a **plastic bag / fire.**

Zero conditional

6 ☆ Match the sentences.

1 If it's hot *c*
2 If fish eat rubbish
3 If it rains
4 If we recycle rubbish
5 If we don't put out fires

a they die.
b we save the water.
c ~~we take the beach umbrella.~~
d it's very dangerous.
e we can help the environment.

7 ☆☆ Order the words. Match the sentences to the pictures below. You draw the missing picture!

1 clean, families beach If the is come .
If the beach is clean, families come.

2 they If rubbish families bring come, .
_____

3 If isn't the leave the rubbish, beach they clean .
_____

4 the isn't clean, families come beach If don't .
_____

8 What does the sign say?

> **Plea set akey ourr ub bi shh om ew ithy ou.**
> _____

9 Circle and correct ten mistakes in the text

H
hi, I'm fred from *the fisherman's boat restaurant*, but I am a fisherman too. We don't have small fish on our menu. If we catch small fish, we throw them back. If we don't, they can't grow, then there are no more fish. We never use food from tins, and we always recycle our glass bottles

our menu is on recycled paper from the Eco-Paper factory. We make bags from our fishing nets. I really hate plastic bags. I see them in the sea especially in july and august. It makes me very cross. If the sea is full of rubbish the fish die

1 Read and complete the sentences below.

> ### Join us!
>
> Help the Go Green Team!
> Help keep our beach clean!
> Have you seen the beach since the storm?
> Have you seen the paper, cardboard, glass,
> and plastic rubbish on the sand?
> Help us pick it up!
> It's dangerous for the animals, the birds and the fish.
> It's dangerous for you too!
> If it's sunny tomorrow, we will meet there at 10 o'clock.
> If you come, you will have a great time!
> Bring a friend too!

1 The beach is dirty today because of the *storm.*
2 On the sand you can see _____ , _____ ,
  _____ and _____ .
3 The Go Green Team want to pick it up because it is
  _____ for _____ .
4 They are going to meet at _____ .

Talking Tips!

2 Choose and write one talking tip for each picture.

1 He's so cute. (Don't be daft!)
2 He's in a rush. Don't be nosey!
3 Watch out! I'm exhausted.

First conditional

3 ☆ Match.

1 If he plays in our team,   *e*
2 If we go to the beach,
3 If I can't come,
4 If we find a bag,
5 If people pick up their rubbish,
6 If they close the cafe,
7 If you don't wear a jumper,

a we'll take the beach umbrella.
b we won't open it.
c you'll be cold.
d we'll be hungry.
e ~~we'll win the match.~~
f the beach will be clean.
g I'll send you a message.

4 ☆☆ Write sentences in the first conditional. Use phrases from the box.

> he won't fall on the rocks   Mia phones
> ~~I go on holiday~~   you're hungry
> we won't go to the cinema   he wears shoes
> they pick up the rubbish   I'll take a message
> ~~I'll send you a card~~   there isn't a good film
> I'll buy you a sandwich   the beach will be clean

1 *If I go on holiday, I'll send you a card.*
2 If _____
3 _____
4 _____
5 _____
6 _____

Look, a bird!

1 *Don't be daft!* If that's a
bird, I'm an elephant!

2 _____

3 _____

5 ⭐⭐ **Read and underline the five sentences that are in the first conditional.**

This morning we arrived on the island of Floreana. The beaches are very clean here, but the rocks are dangerous. <u>If you don't wear shoes, you'll cut your feet.</u> If we have time, I'll send you a card from Post Office Bay. It might take years to get to you! At this Post Office, if people find a card with an address near them, they take it home, then they make sure the right person gets it. There are no stamps and no postmen! If you like, I'll show you some photos.
Tomorrow, if the weather is good, we'll go diving. If we're lucky, we'll see some sharks. I must go. If I'm late for breakfast, there won't be any fruit juice.
Bye!
Patti

6 ⭐⭐ **Write the sentences you underlined in Exercise 6 in a different way.**

1 *You'll cut your feet, if you don't wear shoes.*
2 I'll send you _____
3 I'll show you _____
4 We'll go _____
5 We'll see _____
6 There won't _____

7 ⭐⭐ **What will Tom do tomorrow? Write first conditional sentences.**

1 hot / swimming
If it's hot, he'll go swimming.

2 rain / shopping
_____

3 tired / watch a film
_____

4 meet friends / play basketball
_____

5 not get up late / not miss the boat
_____

8 ⭐⭐⭐ **You have won four tickets. Write sentences about what you will do if you go on the trips. You can use the ideas in the box to help you.**

go to the beach   write a postcard   take photos
eat pizza   watch the fish   jump into the water
take my sister

a trip to Floreana

a ride on a boat

a climbing holiday

lunch in any restaurant that you like

1 If I go to Floreana, I'll _____

2 If _____
_____

3 _____
_____

4 _____
_____

The Magic Amulet

8ᶜ

1 Read. Match the questions to the answers.

At the obelisk, Max and Holly found the entrance to a tomb. They opened the door with the amulet. Inside they saw a terrible mess! Holly said it looked like Max's bedroom. At first they thought it must be rubbish, but it wasn't! There was furniture and pots with food and drink. Max was feeling hungry but didn't eat anything. They found a very heavy treasure box which Max wanted to take. Suddenly they heard a noise. It was soldiers from the palace. Nebi told them where they were.

1 Where did Max and Holly find the entrance to the tomb?   *g*
2 How did the soldiers know they were there?
3 What were the pots for?
4 How did they open the door?
5 Where were the soldiers from?
6 What did Max eat?
7 What was inside the tomb?

a They used the amulet.
b It was full of furniture and pots.
c They were for food and drink
d He didn't eat anything.
e They were from the place.
f Nebi told them.
g ~~It was at the obelisk.~~

2 Order the words and write the sentences correctly.

must be entrance to the It tomb a !
_____

my see it amulet will Let's open if !
_____

Second conditional

3 ☆ Circle the correct words.

1 Holly and Max would dig, if they **had** / **have** a spade.
2 If they **ate** / **eat** the food, they'd be ill.
3 Someone would see them, if they **take** / **took** the treasure.
4 If they **walked** / **walk** quietly, the soldiers wouldn't hear them.
5 If Egypt **is** / **was** closer, I'd go.
6 The soldiers wouldn't be there, if Nebi **didn't speak** / **doesn't speak** to them.
7 If the tickets **weren't** / **aren't** so expensive, I'd buy one.

4 ⭐⭐ Order the words.

1 wouldn't | I | in | light | if | lived | Australia | I | fires | .
If I lived in Australia, I wouldn't light fires.

2 I | if | wouldn't | have | we | bath | had | no | a | rain | .
If _____

3 I'd | rubbish | bins | no | if | my | take | there | rubbish | were | home | .
I'd _____

4 a | if | I | would | didn't | I | bike | walk | have | .
If _____

5 money | boat | if | had | I | a | buy | of | I | wouldn't | lot | a | .
I wouldn't _____

6 we | if | save | recycled | we'd | rubbish | all | planet | the | .
If _____

7 we'd | use | help | the | didn't | plastic | bags | environment | if | we | .
We'd _____

5 Tick (✓) the sentences that you agree with in Exercise 4.

6 ⭐⭐ Use five of the sentences from the box to complete the sentences below. Remember to use the second conditional.

> ~~I had some money~~   I am rich   I saw a jellyfish
> live near a beach   It's going to rain   I see a crab
> It wasn't raining   I am going to find out about it
> I lived in Hawaii   I understood hieroglyphs

1 If *I had some money*, I'd buy it for you.
2 If _____, I'd go for a swim.
3 If _____, I'd learn how to surf.
4 If _____, I'd explain them to you.
5 If _____, I'd run.

Giving advice

7 Match the problem with the advice.

1 I've lost my amulet. *e*
2 The bus is going.
3 I've dropped my sweet wrapper.
4 The sea looks dirty today.
5 The box is too heavy.
6 There's seaweed in my shoes.

a If I were you I'd run!
b If I were you I wouldn't go in.
c If I were you I'd clean them.
d If I were you I'd leave it.
e ~~If I were you I wouldn't tell Ra.~~
f If I were you I'd pick it up.

8 Give the advice for each problem.

1 Oh no, I've dropped the milk!
If I were you, I'd clean up the mess.

2 I can't open the box!
_____

3 I've got a bad headache.
_____

4 I've lost my English book.
_____

5 My bike's broken!
_____

6 The dog isn't well.
_____

8ᵈ Let's Revise!

Vocabulary

1 Match.

1	sweet	a	bag
2	rubbish	b	umbrella
3	beach	c	box
4	plastic	d	wrapper
5	cardboard	e	bin

2 Write the words correctly.

1	gsuelal	4	rulett
2	dnsa	5	cork
3	elhls	6	awedsee

3 Match the phrases and pictures.

1	drop rubbish	5	reuse plastic bags
2	put out a fire	6	pick up rubbish
3	recycle paper	7	light a fire
4	save water	8	switch off the lights

Grammar

4 Write zero conditional sentences.

If have you save a shower you water , .

1 _____

If chocolate cat my ill eats she gets , .

2 _____

If recycle help the environment I rubbish I , .

3 _____

___/20

5 Complete the sentences with the words in brackets. Use the first conditional.

If it is hot on your birthday, ¹_____ (we / go / the beach).
Remember, if ²_____ , (you / not / wear shoes) you'll cut your feet! If they open the café, ³_____ (we / buy / ice cream). If you like, ⁴_____ (we / take / dog).

6 Complete the sentences with the correct verb. Use the second conditional.

1 If I _____ in Africa, I'd _____ baskets out of plants. (make / live)
2 If I _____ the baskets, I'd _____ a bike. (sell / buy)
3 If I _____ a bike, I'd _____ my grandmother. (visit / have)

___/16

Functions

7 Separate the words and match with the problem.

1 I've dropped the glass!

_____

2 I've got a headache!

_____

a Iflwereyoul'dseethedoctor
b Iflwereyoul'dpickitup

___/4

Your score	Your total score
	___/40

31–40   21–30   0–20

9 Parties

My Picture Dictionary

Party phrases

1 Find nine words in the word search and write them in the correct place in column A below. Complete column C with phrases from the box. You can use them more than once.

> the candles   the mess   a present   the decorations   invitations   in new clothes   the dancing   with friends

C	L	E	A	R	O
O	D	A	U	E	B
W	R	A	P	A	L
J	E	G	O	O	O
O	S	E	N	D	W
I	S	T	A	K	E
N	I	P	U	T	A

A	B	C
¹*blow*	out	ª*the candles*
2 _____	off	b _____
3 _____	in	c _____
4 _____	down	d _____
5 _____	together	e _____
6 _____		f _____
7 _____	up	g _____
8 _____		h _____
9 _____		i _____

2 Use the remaining vowels in the word search to complete these phrases.

1	d_o_wnl_oa_d	the m_u_sic
2	pr_ p_re	the f_ _d
3	l_ght	the c_ndles

9ᵃ A Surprise!

1 Complete the dialogue. Use the words in the box.

> ~~present~~ candles card music food sandwiches
> decorations cake

Lily Hi Mia, here's your ¹*present*. I didn't wrap it up, it's inside the ²_____. Here, open it.

Mia Oh, what is it? It's the *Britain's Got Talent* DVD! Wow! Thanks! I can't wait to watch it!

Lily Hey, let me help prepare the ³_____. Is that the cake?

Mia Yes, It's a cheese ⁴_____, but I can't put the ⁵_____ on it, it's too soft.

Lily It looks great. If I were you, I'd put the candles on the ⁶_____.

Mia Don't be daft! Here, help me put up the ⁷_____.

Lily OK. Oh, I wish I was taller! Get me a chair!

Mia Oh, don't worry, my dad can do that.

Lily Cool! If you like, I'll download some ⁸_____?

Mia Yes, please!

Lily Wow, I wish I had your computer!

Mia It's my dad's, but I can use it sometimes.

Dad Mia! No, you can't!

Talking Tips!

2 Complete with the correct talking tips.

> ~~What's up?~~ Go on! It was incredible!
> I'm exhausted!

Seb Hey! ¹*What's up?*

Ryan ²_____ I was at Ziggy's party yesterday!

Seb How was it?

Ryan ³_____ He had a live band.

Seb Wow, that sounds amazing! Can I come with you next time?

Ryan I'm not sure.

Seb ⁴_____ Please!

Ryan Yeah, of course you can!

wish

3 ⭐ Write sentences. Then tick the ones that are true for you.

I My friend My brother My sister My parents	wish wishes	I he she they	had didn't have could was were	a dog more time more money a guitar homework dancing lessons speak better Eng win something older less nervous famous

1 *My friend wishes she had a dog.*
2 _____
3 _____
4 _____
5 _____
6 _____
7 _____

4 ⭐ Deb is getting ready for a party. Complete the sentences. Use the words in the box and the pictures on page 73 to help you.

> ~~knew~~ had love was believe like

1 I wish I *knew* what to get him.
2 I wish I _____ a more fashionable dress.
3 I wish my hair _____ longer.
4 Hey, I _____ your hair! And that's a cool dress!
5 Happy birthday, Jake! Here's your present, I hope you _____ it.
6 I don't _____ it! It's what I always wanted!

Expressing surprise and disbelief

8 Use the words in the box to find four ways of expressing surprise.

> don't ~~amazing~~ That can't be true ~~That's~~ can't believe be I it You serious

1 _That's amazing!_
2 _____
3 _____
4 _____

9 Match Betty's questions with Trevor's answers.

Trevor I wanted to go on holiday and the next day, I won a trip to Hawaii!
Betty ¹_That's amazing, did you go?_
Trevor Yes, and on the plane I met Angelina Jolie.
Betty ² _____
Trevor Yes, of course, she asked me lots of questions.
Betty ³ _____
Trevor Well, she wanted to know about my film.
Betty ⁴ _____
Trevor I know, but I had a DVD in my bag and she wanted to watch it.
Betty ⁵ _____
Trevor Yes, she loved it. It was _Tomb Raider_.

a I don't believe it! Did she speak to you?
b You must be joking! Did you give it to her?
c That can't be true! You haven't made a film.
d ~~That's amazing, did you go?~~
e You can't be serious.
  Give me an example.

---

5 Separate the words. What was Jake's present?

theCDofasongcalledIwishIwasJamesBond

It was _____

6 ⭐⭐ Order the words.

1 | traffic | there | Mum | wasn't | wishes | any | .
Mum wishes there wasn't any traffic.

2 | I | lived | my | wish | a | on | desert | family | island | .
_____

3 | had | Mum | and | they | boat | a | Dad | wish | .
_____

4 | sunny | weather | always | wishes | the | was | and | warm | Dad | .
_____

5 | school | go | My | to | children | didn't | wish | friends | and | I | have | to | .
_____

6 | play | My | guitar | the | day | all | she | sister | wishes | could | .
_____

7 | he | wishes | looked | a | film | like | brother | star | My | .
_____

7 ⭐⭐⭐ What about you? Write what you wish.

I wish _____

1 Read. Think of a title for one of the photos.

I wish I didn't have a birthday on Christmas Day! I always get some extra presents of course, but it isn't the same. We put up decorations for our family Christmas party so there is nothing that says 'Happy Birthday' and my parents wrap up my presents with wrapping paper that has stars and bells on it! I'm not complaining, but I wish my birthday was in the summer!

Becky

Well Becky, my birthday is in the summer. It's on 21 June. Usually, nobody remembers my birthday, they are all too busy celebrating the longest day of the year! Last year was fantastic though. We got together with friends in Avebury where there are some ancient stones. Everybody dressed up and there were fireworks and drums and lots to eat and drink. We all joined in the dancing, and finally we had a cake with candles. Suddenly ... surprise! Everyone started to sing Happy Birthday! They didn't forget after all. It was incredible! I wish my birthday was on 22 June, but I don't wish it was in the winter.

Lea

2 Answer the questions.

1 When is Becky's birthday?
Christmas Day

2 What's special about Lea's birthday?
_____

3 What happens in Avebury on Lea's birthday?
_____

4 When is your birthday?
_____

5 Do you wish it was on a different day?
_____

Adjective suffixes

3 Complete the puzzle with the missing vowels. Finish the sentence below with the middle word.

1	T	H			**G**	H	T	F	U	L	
2		C	H		**L**	D	I	S	H		
3	C		M	F		R	T		**B**	L	E
4				F	A	**M**	O	U	S		
5	D		N	G		R	**O**	U	S		
6				T	T	**R**	A	C	T	I	V	E
7	F		S	H			**N**	A	B	L	E
8						S	**E**	F	U	L	
9	S		L	F		**S**	H				

My grandmother always wears _____ clothes

4 Find three words and complete the sentences.

un ful able sive iev pain en exp bel

1 I can't buy that present because it's very
   _____

2 Her grandmother is so glamorous it is
   _____!

3 The wig was attractive but _____ to wear.

5 Complete the words in the sentences.

1 Do you think birthday parties are child*ish*?
2 Is it glamour___ to be a film star?
3 Are fashion____ clothes too expen____?
4 Do you prefer use___ presents?
5 Is it important to look attract___ at parties?
6 Do you always wear comfort____ shoes?

6 Now answer the questions in Exercise 5. Use the words in the box.

yes no sometimes I'm not sure

Verb + -*ing* or infinitive

7 ⭐⭐ Complete the phrases and write them in the correct column.

enjoy / dress up   plan / have a party
like / open presents   can't stand / play the piano
can't wait / travel   hate / wrap presents
expect / pass my exams   miss / swim   love / dance

verb + -*ing*	verb + infinitive	verb + -*ing* or infinitive
I enjoy dressing up	I plan to have a party	I like opening / I like to open presents

8 ⭐⭐ Read the text. Find two sentences to put in each column in Exercise 7.

Ned, Nick, Tina and Tom are friends. Ned enjoys having parties. He likes to cook and prepares his own party food. Every Saturday he practises making cakes. His friends can't wait to eat them! Tina and Tom can't stand going to parties. They love watching films. They always celebrate their birthdays at the cinema. Nick is different. He always prefers to be outside. Last year, he decided to invite his friends to the water park for his birthday. It was fun. At the end of the day, everybody decided to have an ice cream in the cafe.

9 ⭐⭐⭐ Complete the sentences. Use your own ideas or ideas from the box.

celebrate my birthday   wearing uncomfortable shoes
have a cake   invite my friends   wrapping presents
get a present   eating cold chicken

1 I can't wait to _____
2 I expect to _____
3 I enjoy _____
4 I can't stand _____
5 I plan to _____

The Magic Amulet

1 **Who is speaking? Complete the sentences with the missing vowels and match them to the correct person.**

1 W _a_ i t f _o_ r m _e_! ———————   a   Nebi
2 _'m w_ _ _r_ng the Ph_r_ _h's cr_wn!   b   Holly
3 _ w_nt the p_w_r!   c   Max
4 I c_n't d_ it! It's _mp_ss_bl_!   d   Ra

2 **Find a phrase in Holly's diary that says:**

1 She thinks Nebi is always close.
   I expect to see Nebi everywhere I go.
2 She doesn't like being in Ancient Egypt.
   _____
3 She is scared.
   _____
4 She wants to go home.
   _____
5 She is cross with Max.
   _____

> I can't stand being here any more! Everybody's
> starting to argue and Max is being really childish. He
> showed me a mouse yesterday, and said he's going to
> teach it to speak English. I can't wait to go home. I
> wish I wasn't so nervous. I expect to see Nebi every
> where I go. If I had a wish, I'd be back in the
> museum with Dad.

Verbs with two objects

3 ☆ **Write sentences. Use words from the numbered columns.**

1	2	3	4
Show	Max	the story	to me
Give	the soldier	the crown	to Nebi
Tell	me	the words	to Holly
Pass	Ra	the amulet	to Dad
		the key	

a   1 _Give_   2 _Max_   3 _the key._

b   1 _Show_   2 _the crown_   3 _to Holly._

c   1   2   3

d   1   3   4

e   1   2   3

f   1   3   4

4 ☆☆ **Write each sentence in two different ways.**

1 show / amulet / Holly
   Show Holly the amulet.
   Show the amulet to Holly.
2 tell / Ra / story
   _____
   _____
3 pass / Max / crown
   _____
   _____
4 send / Dad / message
   _____
   _____
5 teach / Nebi / English
   _____
   _____

5 ⭐⭐ **Circle the objects that need *to* before them.**

Holly was scared of Nebi. 'Give **me** the amulet!' he said, 'Give it (me) now!' Holly passed the amulet **Nebi**. 'Now tell **me** who gave it **you**,' Nebi said. Holly didn't reply. Her dad always taught **her** not to speak with strangers. She wanted to send **Max** a text message. She started to write **him**, but it was impossible. Nebi was watching. Suddenly she heard a noise. It was Max. He was telling **her** to wake up!

6 ⭐ **Ask and answer.**

1 pass / Dad ✓
   Could you pass Dad the water?
   Yes, of course.

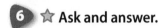

2 give / my brother ✗
   _____ ?
   No, sorry. I can't.

3 send / my parents ✓
   _____ ?
   _____ .

4 show / my sister ✓
   _____ ?
   _____ .

5 teach English / my friend ✓
   _____ ?
   _____ .

6 tell / me ✗
   _____ ?
   _____ .

7 ⭐ **Nebi is leaving the airport when a man calls him back. Circle the correct words.**

Man Good Morning, sir, (show) / open me your bag please.

Nebi Why? I'm in a hurry!

Man ²**Find** / **Give** the key to me please.

Nebi I don't remember where it is.

Man Well, you have to find it, and I don't like ³**waiting** / **to waiting**.

Nebi Oh here it is, in my pocket.

Man Well, ⁴**pass** / **hold** it to me.

Nebi Oh no, it's the wrong one. I lost the other one.

Man You must be joking! Sorry sir, but you will have to ⁵**tell** / **explain** me your story at the police station.

8 **What was in Nebi's bag? Use the underlined letters in Exercise 7 to make the word.**

He was trying to hide _ _ _ _ _ _

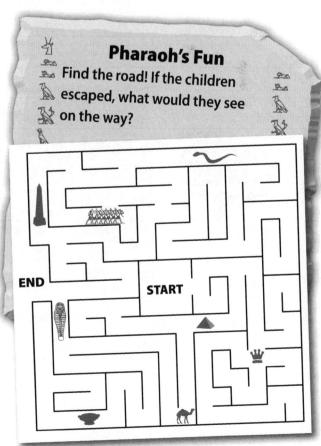

Pharaoh's Fun
Find the road! If the children escaped, what would they see on the way?

END

START

The Invitation

Reading

1 Read, then write down the names of the people, places and dates from the text in the box below.

Every year, since 1929, there has been a very special party in Hollywood. It isn't a birthday party, and you won't see any presents, but it's lots of fun and full of prizes and surprises. The party is for the stars at the Oscar celebrations. Everyone wants an invitation but only a few people get one. The film stars get dressed up in glamorous clothes and the actresses wear their most attractive jewellery.

Rubina Ali was only nine years old when she got her invitation to the Oscar's. She came from a very poor family living in India. Rubina didn't have birthday parties. She didn't know when her birthday was! It sounds incredible, but it's true.

Rubina and her friend Azhar, who also had a part in the film, enjoyed playing in the street and dreaming of a different life. Like most children, they often wished they were famous and that they didn't have to go to school. Rubina never expected to be in a film, or to travel to America. She didn't expect the film to win so many prizes! It wasn't all easy. Every day the children in the film practised singing and dancing and learnt to say their lines. They enjoyed working on the film but missed playing with their friends.

Finally in February 2009 the film arrived at cinemas all over the world. Audiences loved watching the young stars, and soon Rubina and Azhar were famous. After working on the film, Rubina started writing a book about her life. Now she can't wait to study, and to find out what other surprises are waiting for her.

Write three sentences using the words in the box.

Rubina

1 _____
2 _____
3 _____

Writing

2 Imagine that you are going to interview Rubina for a magazine. Write five questions and answers.

You want to know her age and where she's from, what it was like to work on the film and what her plans are for the future.

1 **You** How old _____?
  Rubina _____
2 **You** _____?
  Rubina _____
3 **You** _____?
  Rubina _____
4 **You** _____?
  Rubina _____
6 **You** _____?
  Rubina _____

3 Complete. Use these words.

> ten amazing Oscar us

Tatum O'Neil showed [1]_____ her [2]_____. She won it in 1973, when she was only [3]_____! It's [4]_____ but it's true!

My Picture Dictionary

News webpage

1 Find the words and match to the pictures.

1 ewns ieahdnel *news headline*
2 esnw tysro
3 ievdo lpci
4 mlfi wevrie
5 rethewa ocstfrae
6 lvei bwehtac
7 magse nda dcoswcsorr zpuezls
8 snartcoo dan sjeok
9 temitonoipc
10 tensitvadmree
11 ohpresoocs
12 glob

Telescope for sale!
£100

Star signs

Dancing Cat Wins Competition

1

The winner of this week's In the News video competition is a dancing cat! You can watch the video clip on tonight's programme. You can also watch it on the website. There were hundreds of video clips sent in and it was difficult to decide on the winner.

Cool kitty!

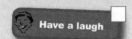
Have a laugh

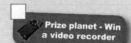
Prize planet - Win a video recorder

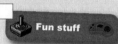
Fun stuff

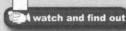
Cinema news – read about the new James Bond

My day to day diary

Chat to Estelle

watch and find out

2 Which part of the news webpage did the children look at this morning?

1 **Mia** It's going to rain this afternoon.
the weather forecast

2 **Tom** There's a really good film on this week.
_____

3 **James** This camera looks great, I'd love to have one.
_____

4 **Zak** Hey! It's my lucky day!
_____

5 **Lily** Wow, I could win a holiday!
_____

3 Complete the sentences with words from Exercise 1, so that they are true for you.

1 I sometimes read _____
2 I never _____
3 I like _____

my words

Do you know more news webpage words? Write them here.

_____
_____
_____

1 **Read and complete the dialogue.**

> ~~advertisement~~ crosswords competition
> horoscope video clip headlines incredible
> famous

Mia Please welcome Lily to our live chat show, *Talk Back*. Hi, Lily! Tell us your story.

Lily Well, I saw an ¹*advertisement* in the newspaper asking for funny video clips for a competition. That morning my ² _____ said if I enter a ³ _____, I will win a prize!

Mia Do you always read your horoscope, Lily?

Lily Oh, yes, of course, and I love the cartoons too, but I can't stand doing ⁴ _____.

Mia Tell us about the competition.

Lily Well, it was all a mistake. I pressed the wrong button on the camera and I didn't know that I was filming.

Mia Ah yes, I do that too sometimes.

Lily Later that evening we watched the ⁵ _____ and we all started laughing. I decided to send it in. I love competitions!

Mia And now you are in the ⁶ _____!

Lily Yes! It's ⁷ _____! I'm going to be ⁸ _____!

DANCING CAT!

2 **Write two sentences about Lily. Use the words in the box.**

> being She competitions Lily doing in
> crosswords likes can't stand

1 _____ .

2 _____ .

Are the sentences true?

3 **Complete the sentences about you.**

1 I can't stand _____

2 I enjoy looking at the _____

Talking Tips !

4 **Find the words and match with the pictures.**

1 eH's os cteu! *He's so cute!* - C

2 uQkci dhei!

3 on'tD eb osyne!

4 hatW rae oyu pu ot?

5 diWkce !

Question tags

5 ☆☆ **Complete the sentences with question tags.**

1 This is Lily's video clip, *isn't it*?

2 She filmed it by mistake, _____?

3 The video will make her famous, _____?

4 Her friends are in it, _____?

5 She's got three cats, _____?

6 ☆ **Now add the answers. Choose from the box.**

> Yes, she did. No, she hasn't. No, they aren't.
> Yes, it is. Yes, it will.

7 **Separate the words to find the answers.**

1 What did Lily win?

HerprizewasatriptoMiamiwithherfamily.

_____

2 What happened in Miami?

Shefilmedanothervideoclipandwonanotherprize!

_____

8 **Order the frames of the video clips.**

Clip 1 ¹*A* ²___ ³___
Clip 2 ⁴___ ⁵___ ⁶___

9 ☆ **Read the sentences and match with a frame from Exercise 8.**

1 You cat looks really scared, doesn't he?   C
2 Hey, they're going to have fight, aren't they?
3 Oh no! Lily's dad can't swim, can he?
4 The mouse won't wake your cat, will it?
5 Lily's dad has always loved fishing, hasn't he?
6 Hang on! That's a crocodile, isn't it?

10 ☆☆ **Lily is showing James her photos from Miami. Add the correct question tag.**

1 Oh wow, that's your hotel, *isn't it*?
2 You had a great time, _____?
3 I'm sure you'll go again, _____?
4 Black Eyed Peas were playing there last summer, _____?
5 They're coming to England soon, _____?
6 Mia's brother can get us tickets, _____?
7 He got us concert tickets before, _____?
8 Oh look, you're wearing that spotty T-shirt that I gave you, _____?

Review of functions

11 **Complete the words with the missing vowels and fill in the table.**

a I'm f*e*d *u*p.
b It m_st b_ the sph_nx.
c You c_n't b_ s_r___s!
d Let's h_v_ _ p_rty!

1	Making a suggestion	
2	Complaining	*a*
3	Expressing surprise and disbelief	
4	Making deductions	

12 **Write a dialogue. Use these sentences and phrases.**

> Why? What's wrong? Sorry, I can't.
> If I were you I'd see the doctor.
> ~~Would you like to come to the tennis match?~~
> I've got a bad headache and my throat hurts.

Tom ¹*Would you like to come to the tennis match?*
James ²_____
Tom ³_____
James ⁴_____
Tom ⁵_____

1 Read the information about Radio Popsicle.
Correct the sentences below.

Join me at Radio Popsicle!

1978: Radio Popsicle started at a hospital in the South of England.
It took a year to build the studio and prepare the team.
1979: The first Radio Popsicle went on the air.
Today, Radio Popsicle broadcasts in The USA, Australia and New Zealand,
as well as the UK.
We need volunteers for two hours a week.
What we do:
We make children laugh when they may be feeling sad.
We organise games and activities. We have fun!
Clowns and magicians are sometimes invited to entertain the children too!
What you would do:
You job would be to help plan and create the weekly radio program.
If you start now you will present the new music programme.
Help us find special guests and interview them on the air.
It's an exciting job, but it isn't for people who are nervous or shy!
Volunteers are chosen by the Radio Popsicle team.
(Next show at Norwood Hospital.)

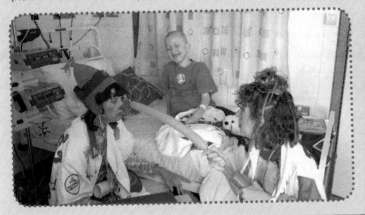

1   Radio Popsicle started in 1998.
    Radio Popsicle started in 1978.
2   It took a year to build the hospital.
    _____
3   They need volunteers for six hours a week.
    _____
4   The volunteers organise maths classes.
    _____
5   Cameramen and technicians make the children laugh.
    _____
6   Working as a volunteer is dull.
    _____

Present simple passive

2 ☆ Match.

1   The programmes are broadcast   *b*
2   Pop stars are interviewed
3   The beds are fitted
4   Games and activities are carefully chosen
5   The sound system is checked every day
6   Volunteers are needed

a   with ear phones.
b   ~~from a studio at the hospital.~~
c   for each age group.
d   to help for two hours a week.
e   by the lucky DJs!
f   before the programme starts.

3 ☆☆ Read. Answer the questions in sentences
using the present simple passive tense.

Every summer the children at Norwood
Hospital have a lovely surprise. They are visited
by a group of clowns called *Abracadabra*! For
more than two hours, the children are entertained by
six clowns and three magicians who bring smiles to
the faces of the children and the nurses too. The tricks
are unbelievable! Rabbits are produced out of hats
and scarves suddenly appear from nowhere. Some
children are chosen to check that the magicians don't
have any secret hiding places.
The show is always filmed by
one of the doctors who comes
to the show. The parents of the
children also come, as well as
other guests from different
parts of the hospital. A good
time is had by all!

1   Who are the children visited by?
    They are visited by a group of clowns called
    Abracadabra!

2   Who are they entertained by?
    _____

3   Where do they produce rabbits from?
    _____

4   What are some children chosen to do?
    _____

5   Who is the show filmed by?
    _____

6   Do the audience enjoy the show?
    _____

People in the media

4 **Find eight words in the word search.**

P	R	E	S	E	N	T	E	R	T
E	D	I	T	O	R	I	D	E	E
A	S	F	D	O	R	T	H	E	C
S	W	R	I	T	E	R	H	O	H
W	A	R	R	E	B	R	A	I	N
C	A	M	E	R	A	M	A	N	I
N	S	T	C	O	R	M	E	D	C
B	Y	S	T	Y	L	I	S	T	I
X	R	T	O	R	A	M	S	G	A
A	J	A	R	T	I	S	T	H	N

5 **Use some of the letters that are left in the word search to make a sentence.**

_____ the volunteers.

6 **Complete the sentences with words from the word search.**

1   The p_resenter_ needs to speak very clearly.
2   We don't need a make-up _____, a s_____
    or c_____ for a radio show.
3   If the film hasn't got an interesting story, they need
    to change the script _____.
4   Choosing the music is part of the music
    d_____'s job.

5   It's important to have a good t_____ to check
    the light and the sound.
6   Talk to the programme e_____ if you don't
    like the show.

7 **Read and answer.**

Programme Editor	Marina Woods
Script Writer	Ed Burns
Cameraman	Nick Robbins
Make-up Artist	Julie Spears
Music Director	Fay Garwood

1   Who was the story written by?   _Ed Burns_
2   Who's got a camera?
3   What did Marina Woods do?
4   Who was the music chosen by?
5   Who made the actors look good?

8 **Cliff is a magician. Sometimes he works with _Abracadabra!_ Tick (✓) the activities Cliff might do to prepare for a show.**

choose tricks ✓
help people to look nice
make-up
read the news
check lights and sound
decide what's on TV
Check out his website!
http://www.cliffthemagician.com/

9 **Use words from Exercise 8 to complete the text.**

Before a show I have to ¹_choose_ the ²_____.
Then I put on ³_____ and my costume. After that I
⁴_____ the ⁵_____ and the ⁶_____.
Finally I am ready and the magic begins!

The Magic Amulet

Tense review

1 ⭐⭐ **Order the words.**

1 are museum now in Holly and the Max .
   Max and Holly are in the museum now.

2 tomb in discovered a Egyptologists The stone a .
   _____

3 crown was a wearing Max .
   _____

4 The Egypt children to been have .
   _____

5 going to is Dad Max tell .
   _____

6 trousers Ra wearing is .
   _____

7 back They go soon will .
   _____

2 ⭐⭐ **Write questions to fit the answers in Exercise 1.**

1 *Where are Holly and Max now?*
2 Who discovered _____?
3 What _____ Max _____?
4 Where _____?
5 Who _____ Max _____?
6 What _____ Ra _____?
7 When _____?

3 ⭐⭐ **Read. Find examples of the following tenses and write them down.**

Today, most children learn about the Egyptians. Tom's class is no different. They have been to the British Museum with their teacher and next week they are going to see a special exhibition in the park. They will see some Egyptian art and learn to make masks. Last year they studied the Romans and made models of chariots in the art class. Tom's chariot is hanging on the wall in his bedroom. It doesn't look like a chariot anymore, because the cat was playing with it!

1 present simple
   Today most children learn about the Egyptians.
2 present continuous
   _____
3 past simple
   _____
4 past continuous
   _____
5 present perfect
   _____
6 future *will*
   _____
7 future *going to*
   _____

4 ⭐ **Complete the sentences use the words in the box.**

> ~~at the moment~~ every day tomorrow
> for an hour already

1 Nebi is very angry *at the moment*.
2 He was looking for Holly and Max _____.
3 The soldiers go out _____.
4 They will probably find them _____.
5 They've looked behind the pyramid _____.

5 ⭐⭐ **Write the sentence numbers in the correct column.**

past	present	future
	1	

1 I swim every day.
2 I'm going to swim in the pool tomorrow.
3 Yesterday I swam in the river.
4 Last night she watched a show on TV.
5 She's going to dance in the show when she's 17.
6 Now she's doing her homework.
7 They're exploring Egypt.
8 Last year they found a tomb.
9 They're going to look for another tomb in the spring.

6 **Remember the story of The Magic Amulet! Complete the pyramid.**

1 **Where?** Where does the story take place?
2 **What?** Name two buildings in the story.
3 **Who?** Write the name of three of the main characters.
4 **Which?** Which animals are in the story. Write down four of them.
5 **What?** What are the objects that are important in the story? Find five and write them down.

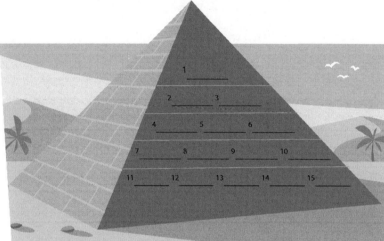

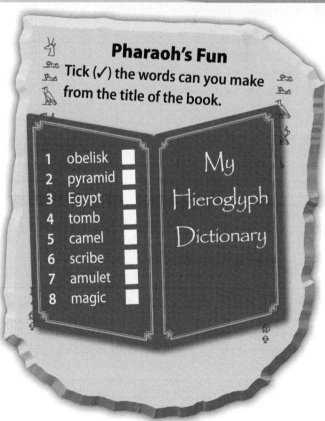

Pharaoh's Fun
Tick (✓) the words can you make from the title of the book.

1 obelisk ☐
2 pyramid ☐
3 Egypt ☐
4 tomb ☐
5 camel ☐
6 scribe ☐
7 amulet ☐
8 magic ☐

My Hieroglyph Dictionary

Let's Revise!

Vocabulary

1 Complete the sections of the news webpage with the words in the box.

puzzle film headline webchat
news weather clip

1 news _____
2 _____ story
3 live _____
4 crossword _____
5 _____ forecast
6 _____ review
7 video _____

2 Separate the words.

blogcartoonsandjokeshoroscopeadvertisementcompetition

3 Circle the correct word.

1 A **technician / presenter** reads out the news.
2 The **make-up artist / script writer** makes sure the people look good.
3 The **programme editor / stylist** decides which programmes are broadcast.
4 The **script writer / music director** chooses the music for the show.
5 The **technician / cameraman** records the programme.

__/17

Grammar

4 Add the question tag.

1 The news isn't very good, _____?
2 The weather forecast was better, _____?
3 Tom checked it last night, _____?
4 We can watch the new film later, _____?
5 They will have it at the video club, _____?
6 You've read the review, _____?

5 Complete the text. Change the words in brackets to the the present simple passive.

The children are making a video of their summer activities. It is a short video so first ideas ¹_____ (brainstorm) and the script ²_____ (write). The video ³_____ (film) on location at the activity centre. The film ⁴_____ (edit) by the summer camp volunteers. Storyboards ⁵_____ (make) and then the video ⁶_____ (send) to all the schools nearby where the teachers ⁷_____ (invite) to show it to the children.

6 Order the words and match with the correct tense.

1 jeans new They're on trying some .
2 yesterday They them bought .
3 don't fit They !
4 to them going the to shop They take are back .
5 shop cheaper They've a found .
6 cooking Dad was weekend last .

a past simple
b future *going to*
c present perfect
d present continuous
e past continuous
f present simple

__/19

Functions

7 Complete and match.

1 Peter is b_r_d with the museum.
2 If I w_r_ him, I'd go home.
3 What's wr_ng with him? He's got a headache.
4 Why d__sn't he wear a hat?

a giving advice
b complaining
c suggesting
d at the doctor's

__/4

Your score | **Your total score**

__/40

31–40   21–30   0–20

Pearson Education Limited
Edinburgh Gate
Harlow
Essex CM20 2JE
England
and Associated Companies throughout the world.

www.pearsonelt.com

© Pearson Education Limited 2010

First published 2010
Nineth impression 2020

ISBN 978-1-4082-0937-0

Set in 12/15pt Myriad Pro Regular and 12/15pt Myriad Pro
Semibold

Printed and bound by CPI Group (UK) Ltd, Croydon CR0 4YY

Illustrated by Andy Peters, Mark Ruffle and Andrew Painter

Photo Acknowledgements
The publisher would like to thank the following for their kind
permission to reproduce their photographs:

(Key: b-bottom; c-centre; l-left; r-right; t-top)

Alamy Images: Paul Doyle 39/2, Eyecandy Images 48 (F), Paul
Gapper 74l, i love images 5, Iconotec 81r, Image Source Black 42
(A), Images of Africa Photobank 46t, Jon Arnold Images Ltd 81l,
Christian Kapteyn 67, Keith Morris 26, 65, Adrian Sherratt 39/6,
42 (F), David Stares 74r, Martin Thomas Photography 48 (E), David
Young-Wolff 39/3, Estelle Zaret 39/4; Camera Press Ltd: WILLIAM
STEVENS / GAMMA / EYEDEA 48 (D); Corbis: © A.M.P.A.S.® FRANK
POLICH / Reuters 78r, Image Source 39/8; FLPA Images of Nature:
Ron Austing 62; Getty Images: AFP 30, Michael Blann / Digital
Vision 39/5, Bridgeman Art Library 84, Kevork Djansezian 78l, PAUL
ELLIS / AFP 39/1, FPG 42b, 48 (C), Ron Levine / Photographers
Choice 39/10, 69b, Bob Thomas / Popperfoto 48 (B); iStockphoto:
42 (B), Nilgun Bostanci 69t, Lachlan Currie 9, Luca di Filippo 69 (key),
Michael Flippo 69 (bag), Justin Horrocks 82r, Andrew Howe 42 (E),
Nathan Maxfield 39/7, 69 (doctor), Vladimir Mucibabic 79br, Serg
Velusceac 79r, Monika Wisniewska 58; Jupiter Unlimited: Comstock
Images 42 (G), Stockxpert 56l, 69 (spanner), Thinkstock Images 42
(C); Maritime Flight Dynamics: 19; Press Association Images: Geoff
Caddick / PA Wire 61, KEVIN P. CASEY / AP 39/9, 42 (D); Rex
Features: c.HBO / Everett 56br, David Fisher 79bl, Lynn Hilton 82l,
Jen Lowery 73, Gary Roberts 46b, Sipa Press 34, Phil Yeomans 35;
Science Photo Library Ltd: Matthew Oldfield, Scubazoo 25; TopFoto:
Kent Meireis / The Image Works 48 (A); www.cliffthemagician.com:
83

All other images © Pearson Education/Martin Beddall

Every effort has been made to trace the copyright holders and we
apologise in advance for any unintentional omissions. We would
be pleased to insert the appropriate acknowledgement in any
subsequent edition of this publication.